D0009345

The Mind of The Market

by the same author

A Critique of Sociological Reasoning

The Mind of The Market

A Study of Stock Market Philosophies, Their Uses, and Their Implications

Charles W. Smith

Rowman and Littlefield
Totowa, New Jersey

To
Gerald D. Weintraub
mentor and friend
in and out of The Market

First published in the United States 1981 by Rowman and Littlefield, 81 Adams Drive, Totowa, New Jersey 07512.

Library of Congress Cataloging in Publication Data

Smith, Charles W., 1938-
The mind of the market.

Includes index.
1. Stock-exchange. I. Title.
HG4551.S6 1981 332.64′2 81-1820
ISBN 0-8476-6983-1 AACR2

Printed in the United States of America

Contents

Preface 6

PART I: THE AMBIGUITY OF THE MARKET
1 What's Going On? 11

PART II: THE TRUE BELIEVERS
2 A Fundamentalist 33
3 An Insider 41
4 A Cyclist Chartist 47
5 A Trader 57

PART III: THE SALESMEN OF THE MARKET
6 The Hard Facts of Market Life 69
7 The Firm Salesman: A Pseudo-Fundamentalist 77
8 The Customer Salesman: A Pseudo-Insider 85
9 The Market Salesman: A Pseudo-Cyclist Chartist 93
10 The Action Salesman: A Pseudo-Trader 99

PART IV: THE MARKET RATIONALIZERS
11 A Market Cynic 109
12 A Believer in the Efficient Market Theory 117

PART V: PUTTING IT ALL TOGETHER
13 The Types through Time 125
14 The Crowd Syndrome: The Followers 133
15 Conclusions: The Uses of Market Knowledge 145
APPENDIX A: Some Practical Advice to the Individual Investor 155
APPENDIX B: A Selected Glossary of Stock Market Terminology 181
APPENDIX C: A Theoretical and Methodological Note 205
Index 217

Preface

This book is concerned with the mind of the market; with the ways the market is viewed, interpreted, and evaluated. It is not a "how to make money" book nor is it an organizational study, though at times it sheds light on both subjects.

The original idea for this study came to me close to twenty years ago when as a graduate student I had my first extensive exposure to the stock market. It was many years later, however, before I felt able to convey my observations and ideas as I wanted; the task of actually doing it and the further research required took some years more.

This long gestation period has had both advantages and disadvantages. On the plus side, I have had the opportunity to observe various types of markets over a considerable period of time; I have been able to test out various ideas in these different types of markets; and perhaps most importantly, I have had the opportunity to benefit from the criticisms and suggestions of a wide range of people. On the negative side, I have at times been overwhelmed by the sheer bulk—to say nothing of the complexities—of the materials which I have accumulated. I have also felt myself pulled this way and that in a desire to speak at the same time to market professionals, individual investors, the lay reader, and professional social scientists—especially sociologists—and about the quite different issues which interest these different groups.

I hope I have been able to solve most of these problems by the range of techniques I have employed to make my story available to all of these groups. First I have tried to minimize the difficulties generated by market jargon while still maintaining an accurate "feel" of the market by including a glossary of stock market terminology (Appendix B), which those unfamiliar with such jargon should find useful. Second, I have tried to avoid going off on various "practical advice" tangents by including another appendix entitled "Advice to the Individual Investor." Finally, to make the study as accessible as possible to non-sociologists I have tried wherever possible to present my more theoretical observations within the narrative context; in the first and last chapters, however, I have addressed some of these issues directly. I have also included as a third appendix a brief theoretical and methological note.

There is another problem related to the relatively long time this book has been in the making which I fear I cannot adequately resolve, namely, the proper acknowledgment of all those who have contributed to making this study possible. All I can do is to thank as a group the literally hundreds of people who gave so generously of their time, trust and expertise even when they must often have seen me as a fairly pestering social scientist. (Those who think I have not sufficiently camouflaged them may be assured that there are many others who are equally convinced that I am describing *them*.) I should also like to thank all of those who read sections and chapters of innumerable drafts and took the time to give me their advice; four, however, deserve special note: David Elkin, Bernice Hoffman, Lynne McFarland, and my publisher, Jim Feather. Sincere thanks are also due to the Warden and Fellows of Nuffield College, Oxford, who made me feel one of the family when as a visiting scholar I was able to finish the study; to my wife, Rita, who has had to read and listen to nearly every word written, respond critically, and then suffer if I didn't like her response; and finally, to Gerald D. Weintraub, who has served as my market alter ego for the last twenty years and to whom this book is dedicated.

One final point. In stressing the "mind" of the stock market, it is not my intention to deny that there are stocks, stock exchanges, stock transactions, rules and regulations which have an existence of their own. There is, of course, the market described by the pamphlets put out by the New York Stock Exchange. These pamphlets describe only the skin and bones of the market; they do not describe the less tangible elements which give life to the market. It is one of the major objectives of this book to explore these elements and in so doing to make sense of the market as it is actually experienced and as it actually functions. In keeping with this objective, we will begin with the market as it is most often seen, namely, as confused, confusing, enigmatic, and paradoxical.

C.W.S.
April, 1981

PART I:

The Ambiguity of the Market

1

What's Going On?

As those who have been around the market for some time often say, "The only thing clear about the market is that nothing is clear." The reason for this is that the market is variously defined; the same event may have completely different meanings for different persons. Most investors have had experiences similar to those in the following dramatization:

Eleven fifteen in the morning—the telephone of our average investor rings. His broker wants him to buy a few hundred shares of a stock that he has been following. The earnings[1] of the company, he tells him, have just come across the ticker and they are up; he thinks the stock is good for a quick twenty per cent move. "Okay", the customer says, "buy two hundred shares."

Three days later, he gives his broker a call. He wants to know how his stocks are doing, especially the new one he just bought. His broker tells him that so far nothing much has happened. He is glad he called, however, because he has another situation for him. Another stock that he has been following has just come out with its earnings and they were down. The stock has sold off a few points and he thinks that it is ripe for buying. It could sell off some more, but he thinks it is time to start nibbling at it. He wants him to buy a hundred shares. He is the expert, our investor tells himself, so he allows his broker to buy a hundred shares at the current market.

Two weeks later he is having lunch with his brother-in-law; they begin to talk about the market. The brother-in-law notes that his broker has been pushing him to buy a particular company which is rumored to have an exciting new product. Our customer gets quite excited because he already owns some shares in the company. That afternoon he calls his broker to see if he thinks that more shares should be bought based on his brother-in-law's rumor. To his surprise, his broker tells him that it would be a good time to sell what he already owns. "You'd be better off putting your money in GHP; it's rumored that ZYX is trying to take them over."

Two days later our friend receives the news letter of a chart service to which he has taken a trial subscription. The service is very bearish. It argues that many stocks are trading in the upper ranges of their normal trading ranges. It strongly recommends selling a significant portion of one's holdings. That same day on the train to work, a neighbor informs him that he is seriously considering taking the recommendation of another chart service which argues that the market is ready to break out of its old trading range and make new highs for the year. Later that morning our customer calls his broker to get his feelings; his broker tells him that he feels that all of the chart services are not worth the paper they are printed on.

As he hangs up the telephone, a feeling of confusion sets in. He asks himself if he's crazy or just stupid. He concludes that if he is going to play the market, he better give it a little more time, since the way things are now, he doesn't seem to understand what's going on. Starting tomorrow, he will carefully read the financial section of his paper; he will even read *The Wall Street Journal*.

The next morning, after checking the prices of his stocks, he reads a long article based upon an in-depth interview with one of the most successful money managers on Wall Street. It's a little difficult to follow all of the arguments, but one thing is perfectly clear; the expert is very bullish. Equally important, our friend feels that he is finally reaching those individuals who know what makes the market tick. Unfortunately, the next day, *The Wall Street Journal* has another article based upon an interview with another market expert who is just as bearish as the first was bullish. When our friend's broker calls that afternoon, he tells his secretary to tell the broker that he is tied up and that he will get back to him later. For the rest of the week, he doesn't even look at the financial pages.

Friday evening he decides to give it another try. With a double scotch he settles down in front of his television to watch Wall Street Week. There are three panelists and a guest speaker, all highly respected market professionals.

Again, there is widespread disagreement, but no one seems to be bothered by it; one would almost think, the way they smile and nod at each other's statements, that they were in agreement. Moreover, whenever it is pointed out that what they said a few weeks ago proved incorrect, they are ready with an explanation which makes it sound as if they had, in fact, been correct. In short, *they* don't seem to be confused.

As the show ends, our friend is totally confused. One day he is told to buy a stock because the earnings are up; the next day he is told to buy another stock because the earnings are down. He is told to sell in response to one good rumor and to buy in response to another good rumor. Some people say that he should sell when stocks are up and others tell him to buy. As far as he can determine, it doesn't make any sense, but then there are all these professionals to whom it apparently does make sense. He sits there asking himself which of them is right. Are any of them right? What is one to make of it all?

The most obvious thing to make of our friend's confusion is that he is an amateur and as such doesn't have the faintest idea about what is going on. However, when we turn to the professionals, i.e., stock brokers, money managers, analysts, etc., we find that they are apt to see the market as ambiguous and as confusing as our amateur friend. If anything professionals tend to be more conflicted, because in addition to trying to understand the market, they must, in one form or another, sell their expertise. Though they seldom admit their uncertainties publicly, these uncertainties clearly emerged in the course of my interviews. Most of the supposedly more sophisticated professionals I interviewed felt that the market didn't know what it was, what it was supposed to be, or what it wanted to be. Since they said it all, I will let them speak for themselves. Since they were guaranteed that their names would not be used, they cannot be identified; I have consequently used pseudonyms. All statements attributed, however, are real.

Harry Silver is a senior partner in a large, primarily institutional, brokerage house. As such he has direct access to one of the most prestigious research departments on Wall Street. What does he think of the market?

"It is a crap game."

"What about all the research that his firm puts out?"

"It helps sell stocks, but it isn't worth the paper it is written on."

Are there any people in the market who know what is going on?

"There are a few, but most of them can't make a living; they either don't know how; or are unwilling, to play the game."

How then do you select the people who you put into the more sensitive positions? How do you decide whether a broker is put into retail sales or is moved into institutional sales where he is expected to be more sophisticated?

"Usually by the school he went to and his social class."

How does all this affect you?

"I wait for the day I can retire."

Do you invest your own money?

"Yes."

What approach do you use?

"I follow the guy in the office who has the hottest hand. I'm the public. I want action."

Doesn't this whole situation bother you?

"Only when I think about it."

Jack Reed is a money manager; he runs portfolios whose values are in excess of four hundred million dollars. What does he think about the market? "Basically a 'no win' situation." How does he cope with such a situation? "By trying to maintain a balanced, diversified position with a fair amount of assets in bonds." Would he ever consider structuring his portfolios as a quasi index fund? "Yes, but I would never admit that is what I had done. If I did, I would be out of a job."

Do you think it is possible to manage money according to one's own best market judgment? "Yes, but the risks are too great; if you are wrong, you are likely to lose the account. It is much safer to give your client pretty much what he wants and what he is likely to get anywhere else. Then, if things go badly, at least you are in good company."

In light of all this, how do you see the market? What is it?

"It is the WPA of the upper classes. It is a place where you can put junior to work and assure him a good living – providing you have the contacts – without having to worry that he is going to screw up the economy or the government. It is a much better system than they have in England where they put him to work in an important position and where he can do real damage."

Do you ever think about getting out of the market?

"All the time. Unfortunately, I doubt that I could make the same living doing anything else. Perhaps the one thing I think about doing most is to buy a seat on one of the smaller exchanges and then just to trade for myself."

In many ways Harry Silver and Jack Reed take opposite positions on the market. Harry Silver is primarily critical of those who think that they understand the market; Jack Reed is more critical of those who are only interested in sales. Still, they agree on many points. Both have a very negative view of most market professionals. The only difference they see between an institutional broker and a retail broker is that the former has a more polished presentation of self. Both also believe that the market is pretty much a hoax. On the other hand, both still retain a very real fondness for the market. Others take even a more critical view; Ben Decker is one such person.

Ben Decker pulls no punches; he doesn't have to. He is eminently successful. Among the numerous companies in which he has a controlling interest is a brokerage firm. He has been around the market for over twenty years and knows it inside and out. What does he think of the market? "It's a sham."

To hear a man who is thought by many to be a Wall Street wizard (Harry Silver and Jack Reed are both successful market professionals, but I doubt that many people would call them wizards) state that the market is a sham is, to say the least, a little disconcerting. I felt that he was kidding me. It would be one thing to point out the flaws of the market, but to publicly state, not just imply, that the whole market is a fraud is something else. It didn't take long to realize that he was deadly serious.

Why does he believe the market is a sham? "Because all theories about how to beat the market are based upon the assumption that there is some body of knowledge which is capable of explaining the market, but such a body of knowledge simply does not exist. The market is too complex. People who think that they understand the market are fooling themselves. There are no exceptions. In fact, those who think they understand the market best – for instance, money managers, institutional types, and market analysts—are generally the biggest fools of all. Most people, at least, know that they don't understand what is going on."

If he truly believed this, how could he buy stocks? He doesn't. He claims that he hasn't bought a stock in nearly twenty years; he buys companies. "Stocks are for the public and people who have nothing better to do with their money." Here he distinguishes between someone who buys a twenty per cent interest in a company and thereby acquires a controlling interest from those who merely invest in stocks. "The market offers great opportunities for the first type because there is no logic to the market; there are plenty of undervalued situations. The latter approach is only for those who have nothing better to do with their money. The market may be a great place for someone to learn about the way our economy and political system works. It is also a place where someone can find excitement. It is definitely not a place to make money."

This attitude colors Ben Decker's view of those involved in the market. "No one knows anything. The only difference between the more prestigious firms and the less prestigious is the amount of veneer. Most prestigious firms are also less likely to try to screw you." He is quick to add that anyone who has been around Wall Street for any length of time knows this. "Why do you think that every RR wants to be something else? They only stick with it because they can't make as much money doing anything else. By and large they're lazy and ignorant. Most of them earn ten times what they could earn doing anything else. If you figure it in terms of the hours they put in, the ratio would be more like fifty times what they could earn doing another job."

If this is the way he feels, why does he own a brokerage firm? "Because it is a great business. Where else can you make as much money with such a small investment?"

As I said earlier, Ben Decker doesn't pull his punches, though actually, he overstates his case. After an hour of listening to him debunk the market, I began to push a little. I told him that I really didn't believe that no one could beat the market. I felt that he could beat the market and that he knew it. Pushed, he admitted that, if he had no alternative, he could make money in the market following a very strict fundamentalist approach. "This doesn't contradict what I have been saying, because if I had the financial resources to invest, I would still be much better off buying companies rather than stocks. Furthermore, if I had to make my living as a broker, I would never be able to generate enough commissions."

I asked him if it would be possible if he had a number of very large accounts. He countered by saying that it would never work. "To maintain large accounts, one must be able to project an image of success, and that requires a large income. The commission structure, especially with discounts, doesn't generate such incomes unless one is willing to do some churning. To maintain accounts worth $25,000,000, for example, a broker must come across as at least a couple of hundred thousand dollars a year man; to maintain $10,000,000 worth of accounts, he must come across as someone earning $100,000 a year. Without churning, the first guy would be lucky to earn $70,000, and the second guy $35,000. On the other hand, if they do churn, then they will no longer be functioning as true fundamentalists. In short, a broker without money of his own would starve if he tried to operate as a true fundamentalist."

He added, "Brokerage firms find themselves in a similar situation. A brokerage firm can't afford to be bearish. They'd go broke. They have to be able to recommend stocks for purchase." Couldn't they do business if they followed a technical approach? "That's the absolute height of tomfollery. The technicians are the high priests of sham; that's witchcraft."

Despite Ben Decker's cynical views, I felt that on one level the market made sense to him. Here I was looking for something analogous to Harry Silver's view that the market was one giant crap game or to Jack Reed's view that the market was the WPA of the upper classes. Ben Decker does have such a vision and it is clearly a more eccentric one.

What has Ben Decker concluded after twenty years in the market? What basic order does the market reflect? "Heterosexuals tend to buy stocks, homosexuals bonds; convertible bond buyers tend to be bi-sexual and short sellers tend to be the true 'machos' of the market." He's quite serious about this. "It all has to do with the degree of security one wants in a relationship. The safe relationship is the homosexual relationship; bonds are the safe investment, etc." He added that a study which dealt with this aspect of the market he would find very interesting.

In concluding our discussion, Ben Decker added that in many ways the market was the height of self-deception. "It is a bunch of people who are trying to fool themselves intellectually. This requires that they attempt to fool others." I asked him if it didn't bother him when he was the object of such attempts. He smiled and answered. "No. I don't take the sham of the market personally."

Norman Walters takes the sham of the market very personally. By and large he shares the negative view of the market that Harry Silver, Jack Reed and Ben Decker hold. There is one major difference. Norman Walters believes that there is an order to the market and that the market can be mastered. To him, it is not just a question of ignorance, it is also a moral question.

Norman Walters is one of the premier money managers of Wall Street. Many run more money then he, but few, if any, have a better reputation. Basically, he is a Fundamentalist though he has incorporated elements from other approaches. Where he differs most from the average money managers is in his cosmopolitan view of the market. He's very concerned with world trends and the general socio-political environment. In short, he's committed to a broad view of the market, and judges the market in terms of this broad view. What has he concluded?

"The market has lost its meaning to most who make their living in it and from it. One can contrast most American market professionals with their Swiss counterparts. I'm not sure that the Swiss experts on average do any better for their clients than the American experts do. There is, however, one major difference. The Swiss see themselves as having a sacred trust. They see themselves as the defenders of their clients' economic freedom. As such, they take great pride in what they're trying to do. They may not always be successful, but they don't doubt their own intentions or objectives. The Americans, in contrast, don't feel this way. The pressures upon them to sell stocks and to perform have made most of them very cynical. In many ways they are too sophisticated. They always have to project an image of themselves as knowledgeable. Most know that it is a false image. As a result, they have lost their self-respect. Many have come to see themselves as highly paid con-men. In most cases, they have even less respect for their colleagues. They don't see themselves as doing anything meaningful or useful. As a result, they are unable to take seriously the very real responsibilities they have. Whatever their intellectual limitations might be, have been compounded by this loss of purpose. As a consequence, they perform more poorly than their limited knowledge itself would dictate. They continue to go through the motions, but most have simply given up."

While all professionals do not see the market as futile and meaningless as those just quoted, it is more the general view than realized. Admittedly, some claim to understand the market; most, if pushed, admit that they don't. This lack of understanding isn't a result of a shortage of "explanations", but of their abundance. Professionals are confused by the same variety of interpretations of what makes the market tick as are lay investors. The only difference between lay investors and professionals is that whereas the lay investor is likely to blame his confusion on his own inadequacy, professionals focus on the contradicitons of the market itself.

Why is the market so contradictory?

The most important roots of these contradictions are the conflicting perspectives different persons have of the market and the different interpretations of market events which these varying perspectives generate.

But why should the market appear so differently to different people given that the market seems so simple and straightforward? Stocks go up when there are more buyers than sellers; people buy stocks which have good earnings and yields; companies make more money when the economy is strong; etc. Furthermore nearly all of this occurs in the public domain. The market is a public auction. There are, moreover, fairly rigid laws to insure that all information bearing on the market and particular stocks be made public as promptly as possible. In short, the market would appear in many ways to be one of the last places one would expect to find conflicting perspectives.

The key to an understanding of this apparent paradox is to recognize that people are seldom, if ever, interested in simply knowing "what" is going on. People want to know what is going on in order to know what is going to happen so that they can adjust their own actions to serve their own interests – whatever these interests might be. Knowledge serves as a guide to action.[2]

For knowledge to serve as a guide to action, however, it must tell us more than what is going on; it must also tell us something about why and how what is happening, is happening. This, in turn, requires a more general theoretical grasp of the situation; the apparently simple account of what is happening must take into account and reflect the underlying structure. Different assumptions regarding this underlying structure generate very different accounts of 'what' is happening. How does one know, for example, whether there are more buyers or more sellers? The tape doesn't record "buy" and "sell" orders – it merely records transactions. There are hints: Did the transaction occur on an "uptick" or a "downtick"? In the end, a judgment is still required.

Similarly, how is one to know whether the earnings and/or yields of companies are good. Are the earnings, for example, likely to continue? Has the company juggled their books? Again judgment is required. Determining how a stock is "acting" or the effect of the economy on a specific company is also a question of interpretation.

Here it may be asked whether it is not true that all situations are subject to this process. The answer is obviously yes; all "reality" is an interpreted reality. What makes the market a more extreme case of a general phenomenon is the peculiar feedback character that such interpretations have in the market. As a result the market has a "self-fulfilling prophesy" character which is greater than that of most other situations. To give a concrete example:

Let us assume that we are asked to judge the relative value of two automobiles: A and B. Let us similarly assume that for various reasons we have a bias for A. We judge A better. We can now also assume that if we drove both cars, we would tend to play up the good points of A and play down its bad points; in contrast, we are likely to do just the opposite with car B. In short, there is likely to be a self-fulfilling prophesy aspect to the way we experience the two automobiles. This aspect, however, will not change the mileage we get (though it might shade it a little), prevent a major breakdown, or stop the car from rusting. In the case of stocks, however, such predilections can have the equivalent effect. If enough people think that a stock should be valued higher, they can by active buying push the price of the stock up thereby fulfilling their original definition. In fact, I know of no place where the "definition of the situation" so directly and dramatically affects the situation being defined as does the stock market. It is just this quality that makes the market such an excellent area for analysing the impact of different orientations.

Obviously the market doesn't conform to everyone's definition. If the market did what everyone thought it was going to do, we would all be millionaires many times over. The market responds to consensual definitions; it tends to conform to expectations which are held by numerous individuals.[3]

In light of the numbers of people involved in the market – over 40,000 registered representatives to say nothing of other market professionals and approximately 30,000,000 individual share owners – coupled with these persons' different interests and objectives, it may seem ludicrous to assert that such a consensus is possible. Actually, however, such consensuses are not only possible but quite normal. The reason is that "defining the situation" and/or the "construction of social reality" is a social process not an individual process. There are both concrete and theoretical grounds for this. To begin with the more theoretical: whatever other benefits may be derived from imposing a meaningful order on the world, the first and foremost benefit is that it provides a basis for social solidarity. Put a slightly different way the prime value of any meaningful view of anything is that it can be shared and hence can serve to unite people. At the more concrete level, meanings are the product of social interaction; man does not create a meaning on his own. Moreover, these patterns of social interaction are usually highly structured with a group of experts of some sort playing central roles in maintaining the group consensus.[4] These experts are the market professionals, such as stockbrokers, stock analysts, money managers, financial reporters, etc. This is not to imply that lay investors have no impact on what the market does or how it is interpreted; it is only that any impact is generally filtered through the perspectives of the professionals. Even when a non-professional has an insight of his or her own, the insight is molded to conform to a professional orientation of some sort.

What then are these professional orientations?

(1) The Fundamentalist/Economic view;
(2) The Insider/Influence view.
(3) The Cyclist/Chartist view;
(4) The Trader/Market Action view.

Each entails what can only be called its own basic "vision" of the market.

The Fundamentalist/Economic view stresses the underlying economic conditions affecting individual companies, industries and the general economy of both the United States and the world in general.

The Insider/Influence view, in contrast, focuses upon the supply and demand factors influencing stock prices with special interest given to those individuals and institutions which exert a disproportionate influence on the market in general.

The Cyclist/Chartist view, perceives the market primarily in terms of its own patterns of behavior. It concentrates on past patterns, seeking to discover the patterns of the future.

The Trader/Market Action view, notes the market

movements of individual stocks and the market as a whole. It is concerned with how specific stocks respond to specific information and overall market trends.

Why these four? Why not more? Why not fewer? Why not others?

For one reason because that is the way things are. A better, more theoretical explanation is that each of these overviews reflects one of four basic intentional modes which govern human action in general. The Fundamentalist/Economic view reflects what could be called the external/physical world-pragmatic perspective; the Insider/Influence view is the social relationship-political-argumentation perspective; the Cyclyst/Chartist the symbolic meaning-ordering perspective; and the Trader/Market Action view the experience-emotive-intuitive perspective. It is the peculiar "self-fulfilling prophesy" character of the stock market which allows each of these modes full development and existence in the market in contrast to most other social situations which favor one or another mode over the others. (We shall have an opportunity to return to this issue later.)

How these general overviews are embodied in the specific views and behaviors of individual market professionals is a more complex issue. To begin with, few individuals are completely consistent to any single overview. This is related to another, more important point, namely, that professionals use these overviews for different purposes. While nearly all market professionals, for example, have some interest in understanding the market, those who are primarily interested in understanding the market in order to master it constitute a distinct minority; I call these goal orientated intellectuals the "true believers."[5] Most market professionals, in contrast, are primarily concerned with selling stocks; there are also others who are primarily interested in "explaining" the market and others who just like being "part of" the market. Even here one must be careful not to be too strict since most market professionals have elements of each type, though in most cases one type is usually dominant.

In attempting to come to terms with these various overviews, however, it is best to start with those I call the true believers. The reason for this is that the salesmen, explainers, and players are all constrained by the views of the true believers since it is they who actually are engaged in the process of defining the market while being engaged in the market. The salesman is interested in the meaning of the market only as it allows him to project an image of understanding which he needs to sell stocks; the explainer is interested in the meaning of the market only as they constitute the material with which he must work in order to produce an acceptable account whereas the player is interested in the meaning of the market primarily to tell him where he is and where he was. Put slightly differently, the views of most market professionals are only fuzzy reflections of the articulated views of the true believers. Only after we get to know these true believers will we be able to understand the ways others use these overviews.

Determining whether a particular market professional is or is not a true believer, unfortunately, is often difficult for the reason just given, namely, that many non-true believers sound like true believers; they use the rhetoric of the true believer in selling stocks and/or in attempting to "explain" why things happened the way they did. This is not a point which need concern the reader here; hopefully, by the time he or she has completed this study, they will be able to distinguish the genuine article from the imitations. For now I will take the liberty of introducting four true believers, a spokesman for each of the four general overviews noted above. Once we have heard a little from each, we will attempt to get to know them better.

The scene: a corner table in a Wall Street restaurant.
The time: approximately 1:p.m.
The actors: John, Hank, Bill and Bob.

John: You know, I really like the action of ABC; the market is down two points this morning and it is up a half on some pretty good volume.

Hank: Yup. I heard that Fidelity was taking a pretty big position; I also hear that one or two banks who were unloading it have completed their sales.

Bill: I think that both of you guys are crazy. How can you buy a company that is still trading at twenty-five times earnings in a market like this?

Bob: I don't know Bill, maybe John and Hank have a point. It hasn't really broken its support level throughout this decline. My charts indicate that if we get any sort of market it would be good for 10 or 20 points before it runs into any sort of real selling pressure. Personally, I'd rather try DEF. Its chart looks even better.

John: Bob, I don't care what your charts say. DEF is down another two today and it hasn't lifted at all when the market has.

Hank: I don't know, John, maybe Bob is right. I heard that two different houses will be putting out a strong buy recommendation on the whole integrated circuit industry and at least one of them will highlight DEF. On the other hand, the word is that some insiders have been lightening up on their holdings.

Bill: I don't see how DEF is any better or worse than ABC. They are both trading at such high multiples and for all practical purposes they both pay nothing. How can you mess around with them when there are hundreds of solid companies yielding eight and nine per cent and trading at under ten times earnings to say nothing about the yields you can get on some bonds.

John: You might be right about the bonds, Bill, but most of those stocks you are so hot on are real dogs. One or two of those secondary stocks you follow have been behaving better, but most of them have shown me nothing for months. Admittedly one of those small steel companies you follow has me a little interested – it has lifted nicely on each of the last few rallies.

Hank: If you knew what I've been hearing John, you

wouldn't mess around with any of the steels. There are supposedly two or three pension funds that are up to their necks in steel. They plan to be liquidating them for the next six months. I hear there's a big block overhanging big steel right now.

Bob: Hank may be right. The charts on all the steels indicate that they're stuck in a very tight trading range. Even the one or two that have lifted haven't been able to break out. If you want to go with low P/E stocks with a good yield, I've got a few that look really good to me. They could all be good for twenty per cent moves. Not only do their charts look good but all of them usually do very well at this time of the year.

John: Bob, I've seen your charts, but I don't know how you can touch any of those stocks; they never trade in any volume. It will cost you two or three points to take even a modest position in any of them and God help you if you ever want to get out fast.

Hank: I'd go along with John in all cases except for one. I saw where XYZ is starting to get some institutional sponsorship. Two or three of the big boys have been nibbling at it for the last two months. However, the funds won't touch most of them.

Bill: If any fund touches XYZ, they're crazy. After Bob mentioned it last week, I got hold of its annual statement and its 10-K form. If you checked out footnote 6, you'd see that they're going to have to raise at least three million dollars in the next few months to cover some notes coming due. I hate to think what interest rate they'll have to pay in this market.

Hank: You're scared of your own shadow, Bill. Believe me, if those guys are putting their money in, they must know that XYZ is going to get the necessary loan. One of those institutions had two of their top analysts down at the home offices of XYZ last month for three days going over the company from top to bottom. There must be something good going on down there if they decided to make a commitment.

John: Sure. They figure that if they buy 10,000 shares of that dog, they can drive it up five or ten points. On their quarterly statement, it will make them look awful smart. Just let them try to get out.

Bill: Look, John, as far as XYZ is concerned I agree with you. It is a crummy company, but why are you always so worried about getting out? If you buy good companies with solid earnings and a good dividend, you can always afford to hold them. By buying such companies and holding them, you'll end up doing better than with all this in and out stuff of yours.

Bob: I should be honest with you guys. XYZ is my stock and I think both John and Bill are wrong, but if it rallies through 22, I'll probably sell it since it hasn't been able to hold above the low twenties for years.

John: Well, I'll tell you, Bob, if it came through 22 in volume, I'd be tempted to buy it despite what Bill says. Till then, I'd rather stick with those companies that are showing me something right now. Hey, it's quarter to two. I better get back and see what's happening. I have a feeling that the volume should pick up this afternoon.

Hank: I've got to run too. I've got a meeting with a guy over at one of those new hedge funds. I'm interested in finding out what they are up to.

This stylized discussion reflects the four general overviews noted earlier. Bill favors the Fundamentalist view; Hank, the Insider view; Bob, the Cyclist view; and John, the Trader view. But are these men real? Yes and no. They are what sociologists call "ideal types"; that is, each is a prototype based on a number of similar individuals. During the last sixteen years, I have met a number of Bills, Bobs, Hanks, and Johns. To protect their anonymity, which was guaranteed and to convey a more accurate feel for the market, I have elected to present these "flesh and blood", though "fictional" characters rather than a set of statistical findings. In each case, I have focused upon one such individual, but have camouflaged his personal characteristics by using specific traits of other adherents of the same view. All direct quotes and stated opinions, however, are authentic.

So far, we have had only a quick glimpse of each character. It's time we got to know them and their views of the markets better. It should be remembered that the market professionals to be described – persons with clearly articulated views of the market – are relatively few in number. Once we know the true believers better, we shall take a closer look at the other types.

PART II:

The True Believers

2

A Fundamentalist

Bill Chester has been in the market for over forty years. He started out in the back office of one of the street's major firms during the thirties, and has been a registered representative since the late thirties. Even before joining his first firm, with which he is still associated, he followed the market and has clear memories of the 1929 crash. Today he's a well-established, highly-respected broker. From the first moment we meet him, we know that we are dealing with a successful businessman. His suits are conservative but expensive; his hands are well manicured and his manner is one of confidence. He talks quietly, but it's clear that he is not in any way meek.

I was introduced to Mr Chester by one of the managing partners of his firm. I doubt whether he would have granted me an interview if I had approached him directly. Once it became clear that I knew something about the market, he talked to me freely. In fact, he adopted an almost paternal interest in what I was doing. As I got to know Mr Chester better – I never did get to call him Bill – I realized that his paternalistic style was not limited to his relationship to me. It was a style he used with most of his customers and even his fellow brokers.

Mr Chester is a Fundamentalist. Others see him as a Fundamentalist and he sees himself as one. To Bill Chester, market values reflect economic values. This general orientation determines how he sees the market, individual companies, what he reads, who he talks to, and the stocks he buys. It also determines how he perceives his own role as a registered representative.

To Bill Chester the best indicator of the market as a whole is the Dow Jones averages. The "Dow" tells you where the real market is. It doesn't bother him that the averages are heavily weighted in favor of established "blue chip" companies – It is specifically because they are so weighted that he likes them. He wants little or nothing to do with small untested companies. He doesn't, for that matter, want much to do with large tested companies which trade at high multiples. He's interested only in those companies whose market values are supported by "assets". His bible is Graham and Dodds *Security Analysis.*

Although Bill Chester is primarily interested in the fundamentals of the companies in which he invests, he has great interest in the economy of the country as a whole. He pays a good deal of attention to general economic indicators and to government policy. These concerns are reflected in his reading habits. He reads both *The New York Times* and *The Wall Street Journal* daily. Interestingly, if he could read one paper only, he would read *The New York Times.* In this he differs from the majority of fundamentalists but his preference is consistent with his concern for general economic news, which he sees as more important in the long run than strictly financial news.[1]

Each week, in addition to his daily papers, he reads *Time, Newsweek, Barrons* and *US News and Reports;* he also subscribes to *Fortune* and *Forbes.* Each weekend he sends away for numerous financial reports on individual companies. However, he has little use for any "market service". He doesn't keep or follow any charts, nor does he concern himself with most technical indicators, though he does check the 'confidence index' in *Barrons.* If he were restricted to one weekly publication, he would unhesitatingly pick *Barrons.*

His attitude towards *Barrons* reflects his attitude towards the market as a whole. The first thing he reads is the editorial page; after this he carefully reads the reports on the individual companies featured that week. The rest of the magazine he skims.

Although Bill Chester absorbs a tremendous amount of information, he seldom acts on this information immediately. This is consistent with his view of his own role. He sees himself primarily as a financial advisor whose job it is to digest and interpret information. The information must be of a specific type – namely, fundamental economic and political information. He believes that he must first develop a feel for the economy and the market as a whole. If he has a positive feel, his next job is to pick those solid companies which he thinks are likely to perform as well, if not better, than the market as a whole.

Bill Chester knows that his approach differs from that of most other brokers, especially younger brokers. This doesn't bother him, though during the last forty years he has been upset when his more speculative colleagues have made money and he hasn't. As far as he's concerned, his more speculative colleagues are playing Russian Roulette; to make things worse they're doing it with other people's financial lives. He is fond of talking about "yesterday's hotshots" who were wiped out when the market turned against them.

This is not to imply that Bill Chester is a loner; he's not. He maintains close contact with other brokers and watches carefully what his own firm and other firms are recommending. He also actively solicits the opinions of his more well connected customers. He is only concerned, however, with certain types of information and even then he insists on analyzing it for himself. It is in his relationship with his customers that this aspect of Bill Chester's style is most prominent.

Bill Chester has a fairly high regard for most of his customers' market intelligence; he thinks most customers are smarter than most brokers are willing to admit though he acknowledges that his customers are probably more sophisticated than the average investor. Most of his customers, especially the most active ones, are successful businessmen though it is not their business success per se which Bill Chester finds important. Neither does he give much weight to their abilities to interpret the "tape" or their familiarity with market jargon. He bases his judgments on their understanding of fundamental economic factors and their access to "good" information. He is interested in knowing what the earnings picture looks like to someone in close contact with a company. This does not mean he takes such information at face value, but it is the type of information he feels that he can use.

Bill Chester's customers give him more than information – they provide him with his living. Like most brokers, he works on a commission basis. This can create strains for a Fundamentalist since his approach generates less turnover of stocks than do other approaches. The Fundamentalist generally buys stocks for the long haul. A successful Fundamentalist, consequently, requires customers with substantial sums of money to invest; furthermore, it is preferable that they regularly have new money to invest. Without such large sums, Bill Chester can't begin to earn the commission dollars he requires for his own lifestyle and for the requisite "image of success"; as it is, he must also rely on his own investments. Similarly, it is only customers with large sums of money who can profit tax-wise from long-term investments in contrast to short-term trades. There is, in short, a symbiotic relationship between the Fundamentalist's approach and the needs and resources of customers with substantial economic resources.

Bill Chester feels that the main problem with most customers is that they are lazy; they are not willing to put into the market the time and effort required. Many have sound instincts, but few have developed their critical abilities. As a result, he finds that most of his customers follow his advice quite closely. This does not mean they follow him blindly. To sustain their confidence in him he must make his position understandable to his customers. He would be happier if his customers were more knowledgeable than they are.

Bill Chester has a few trading accounts for which he acts solely as an executor of orders. As he told me, "For them I can't be of much help", though he certainly is not negative towards them. Not only do they generate sizeable commissions; he also feels that most of them know what they're doing. He readily admits, though it is not his style, that some people can make money trading. He is similarly more than willing to handle accounts of individuals who invest on their own, usually as a result of their own information. In these cases he will try to find out why the customer is investing in the particular stock. It's the type of information he finds useful. Questioned about this, he informed me that many of his wealthier clients maintain accounts with other firms. As a result, Chester is able to gather information about the thinking of other professionals with whom he does not have direct contact.

Bill Chester does not feel that all of one's moneys should be invested in stocks. His fundamentalist orientation leads him to look favorably upon numerous other forms of investments, such as bonds, real estate, and insurance. He himself had substantially more sums invested in real estate during the late sixties than he did in stocks. Furthermore, he is negative toward stock options, lettered stocks, and short selling. The ideal investment for Bill Chester is an undervalued stock of a major American corporation.

Despite being negative toward "tips", charts, and short-term trading, Bill Chester is not above using them; but he uses them primarily to guide his selling, not his buying. If he hears a "tip" on a company he owns he is likely to be a seller if it has a substantial move. Similarly, he's likely to be a seller of a company he owns if it begins to run up after making a new high on some chart or if it becomes a favorite of the traders. In such cases, his view is that the stock is being pushed up by speculative fever which cannot be maintained over the long run. Bill Chester believes in the preservation of capital. If it comes to a choice between speculative gains and protection of capital, he will always favor the protection of capital.

From what has been said, it should be clear that Bill Chester takes the long view toward the market. He's never in a great rush to buy or sell. This is reflected in the way he makes his recommendations. While he uses the telephone constantly, as do all brokers, he relies more upon the mail than most established brokers. He sends out hundreds of written reports to his own customers. He is then likely to tell his customers to think over a recommendation and to give him a call if they are interested. Furthermore, when selling, he is likely to make use of limit orders, that is he is likely to offer his stock at a specific price rather than at the present market price. When questioned about this practice, he told me that he only buys "undervalued" stocks and is not about to lose an opportunity for a half a point; on the other hand, when he's selling he wants to get what he thinks the company is worth. Since he doesn't aim to get the top price (he's willing to sell when he feels a company is fairly priced) he doesn't worry about losing his opportunity to sell. There is the added fact that his selling tends to be more intensive than his buying.[2] Here he admits to being a better buyer than seller, but this seems to be a general attitude of most brokers. Whereas some brokers tend to kick themselves for selling too soon, Bill Chester seldom does. As far as he's concerned, the risks involved in obtaining those last few points are just too great.

In many ways Bill Chester would be the ideal broker for widows and orphans. He's both conservative and thoughtful. Unfortunately, there are few widows and orphans who are likely to obtain his services unless they have substantial financial resources; moreover, he feels more comfortable dealing with established businessmen since they can afford the risks that are entailed in the market. Also, these businessmen are the ones who can provide him with the types of information which he requires. It's doubtful that he would refuse any account, even if it were small. Such an account would be less likely to receive the type of attention that Bill Chester gives to his larger accounts.

While there are only a limited number of Bill Chesters, nearly all brokers have little of Bill Chester in them since it's impossible to operate in the market without having some concern for the fundamentals of the marketplace. To Bill Chester the fundamentals of the market *are* the market; the rest is an enigma which is best ignored. As he says, "I don't try to mastermind the market. I am content to look for sound values and to stick with them till the market recognizes them."

This attitude tends to reinforce his general conservative outlook. He is not, however, passive. Bill Chester believes in hard work. At this point in his life, most of this hard work entails going over company reports, talking to people, and keeping up-to-date on all sorts of financial information. Even now, he's usually at his desk before eight in the morning and stays till five in the afternoon. Furthermore, while he refuses to talk business during the weekend, he puts in a good number of hours of reading. When he was younger, he also spent a fair amount of time on the road visiting companies, speaking to administrative and financial officers, checking out plants, etc. He doesn't do much of this now, primarily because of his age.

This explains why Bill Chester is not now as interested in small companies as are a number of other Fundamentalists. It is probably fair to say, in fact, that most Fundamentalists are interested in such small companies. The reason is not hard to understand; small, unknown companies are more likely to be undervalued in a purely economic sense. Bill Chester knows this, but like any true Fundamentalist he also believes that all such companies must be checked out in person – which he is no longer willing to do.

Bill Chester differs from most other true Fundamentalists, or at least market Fundamentalists, in other ways. To begin with, he is more interested in general economic and political events than market Fundamentalists who give greater attention to the economic conditions affecting specific companies and industries. He also differs from most market Fundamentalists in how he makes his living. Bill Chester is a retail broker whereas most true Fundamentalists tend to be market analysts, financial advisors, or institutional brokers for the simple reason that it's difficult for a retail broker to make a living as a true Fundamentalist – he can't generate enough business. Bill Chester can afford to put his customers into bonds and longterm situations because he has substantial assets of his own; most retail brokers don't and consequently can't.

Bill Chester also differs from most true Fundamentalists, and brokers in general, in the respect he gives to *his* customer's opinions. After all, he has managed over a period of years to acquire a comparatively successful and sophisticated clientele. Most customers, he believes, are lazy, uninformed, and simply ignorant of how the market works.

There's one other aspect of Bill Chester's view of himself that deserves some comment. He takes seriously his role as financial advisor. In this respect, he's more like the old time family banker – most of whom were also Fundamentalists – than today's Fundamentalists. Most have been sufficiently burnt by what they consider to be the greed and ignorance of their clients that they have lost their sense of responsibility. They are content to present their information and to make their recommendations, and if people want to ignore what they have to say that's their business. Bill Chester feels, on the contrary, that it's his job to convince his customers that he's right. This is why he attempts to educate his customers as best he can.

There is another important aspect of Bill Chester's attitude toward the market which should be noted. Despite his forty years in the market and his success in it, and his love for it, Bill Chester isn't wedded to the market. When asked whether he has ever thought of getting out, he answers, "All the time."

Nearly all true Fundamentalists, when asked that question, give a similar answer. To the true Fundamentalist, the market is only one element within a broader, more encompassing economic system. Most true Fundamentalists I have interviewed indicated a secret longing to run a business of their own. Many are put off by what they see to be the speculative nature of the market; some are actually morally offended that people are able to make money investing in stocks which are intrinsically overvalued. Most are quite happy when such persons get battered, and if the person had previously made a lot of money, they are often ecstatic. The world of business, and in some cases the academic world, exert a strong pull on many true Fundamentalists; they are seen as places where the Fundamentalist credo is held in higher respect and where its true believers are more esteemed.

3

An Insider

Henry Strong has been involved with the market for approximately twenty-five years. He was commissioned into the army upon graduation from college during the Second World War; he then spent a few years in Washington assigned to the Pentagon in the field of military procurements. He retired as a Lieutenant Colonel in 1948 and went to work for a large aircraft company. He says his work was primarily in public relations, but from some of the things he says, it's quite clear that he was primarily a lobbyist. In the early fifties, he joined an institutional house as a defense industry analyst, but switched within a few months to institutional sales.

Hank – Henry Strong is Hank to just about everyone – asserts that as a young man, he had no interest in the market. He had a very successful uncle whom, he recalls, was very much involved with the market. This uncle owned a successful hardware company, but he spent more time playing the stock market than running his company. Hank remembers his uncle always talking to him about the market, but claims that he never paid much attention to what his uncle had to say. He didn't develop any real interest in the market until he started to work for the aircraft company – some stock options came with the job. Soon, he found himself spending time trying to figure out why his options went up one day and down the next. This led to his more general interest in the market and his decision to become a market professional.

Hank has done very well during these last years. He hasn't acquired the personal assets of Bill Chester, but he makes a very good living. This is reflected in his well-dressed, well-groomed, if somewhat flashy appearance. It's also highlighted by the expensive cigars which he's always offering.

Hank describes himself as a conduit of information. In a very real sense that's what he is. As an institutional salesman, his job is to bring the analysts of his firm into contact with the analysts of the funds, banks, and trusts with whom he deals. Hank's self image, however, differs from that of institutional salesmen who see themselves as peripheral to the market; they are there to provide a specific service.[1] Hank sees what he does, in contrast, as central. To Hank, the market lives on information and information is his game.

As far as Hank is concerned, the so-called underlying value of a company doesn't mean much. The only thing that matters is sponsorship. "It doesn't matter how much money a company makes; it only matters how much people are willing to pay for it." Once over a drink, he confided: "I deal with the best analysts in town. Every week I get a dozen or so reports; some of them run over a few hundred pages. And you know what? They are wrong as often as they are right."

This doesn't mean that Hank is uninterested in what the analysts, or at least some analysts, have to say. The secret is to focus on those analysts who swing some weight. If he can by-pass the analysts entirely and find out directly what the "boys with the money" are going to do, so much the better. He's quick to add that it doesn't always work out. "More than once, I thought I had the inside track on a stock, only to find out that there were bigger guns on the other side."

During the last few years, Hank has focused upon those factors which he feels affect the supply and demand forces at work in the market. His bread and butter remains the information that he is able to acquire through his many contacts. He's developed a keen interest in bond yields because they compete with stocks, net redemption figures of various mutual funds because they indicate the amount of public money involved in the market, and even the international money scene because it reflects funds flowing in and out of the United States. If he didn't have so much time and energy already invested in his personal contacts, he asserts that he would give these factors even more attention. As it is, he plans to do more work in this area in the future if he has the time.

Hank's interest in these factors is, however, more theoretical than actual. He is quick to point out, for example, that it is difficult, if not impossible, for him or anyone else to get an edge when it comes to these things. "There may be some people who can get this type of information early, but I haven't run into any of them yet." There's the added fact that while he "knows" that these factors affect the overall supply and demand for stocks, it is very difficult to figure out how specific facts affect specific stocks. Hank is destined, as a result, to rely in the future as he has in the past upon his contacts. He's also more at home working with people than with written reports.

Hank's "auction" view of the market directly influences the way he looks at a number of other things. He's very down on the small investor. It is not that he thinks they are stupid; it is just that the market is stacked against them. "In the market, there has to be a buyer for every seller and a seller for every buyer. The little guy almost by definition is forced to work against the big boys. The little guy might be right, but the big boys have the money. This is more true today than ever before. As a result, most small investors just can't win." He doesn't have a much higher opinion of professionals, especially retail brokers. "They're just as much in the dark as lay investors."

I was especially interested in Hank's attitude toward market manipulation. Here Hank tends to hedge. "In the old days, there was a fair amount of it; moreover, if you had an inside track you could do pretty well. Today, you really can't. There are some small companies that can still be manipulated, but with all the regulations it's impossible to do it with any of the major companies and it is the major companies with which I have to work when dealing with large institutional accounts."

This attitude is directly related to Hank's pet peeve. When asked what he dislikes most about the market, he quickly answers "government regulation". He feels that such regulations are fine insofar as they limit outright manipulations, though he has his doubts as to how successful they are. On the other hand, he feels they unfairly tie his own hands. He doesn't see where there is anything wrong with someone taking advantage of information acquired by hard work. "Anyone could do what I do if they wanted to put the time and energy into it. Here I am out there hustling and some guy who just sits back and waits gets the information as soon as I do."

His resentment against the government is also based on what he feels is the excessive power of the Federal Reserve. He feels that by controlling interest rates and the supply of money, the Fed has too much influence over the market. "I wouldn't mind so much if their decisions weren't political in nature. They (the Fed) don't juggle things to make a pile for themselves, but the results are pretty much the same."

Despite all of his reservations, Hank is still out there hustling. Unlike Bill Chester, Hank spends relatively little time at his desk. He averages at least two or three appointments a day. Usually it's a lunch meeting or a dinner meeting. More often than not they are social rather than formal meetings. At least three or four nights a week he entertains someone, and when Hank entertains, he does it right. During an average year, he spends more on entertainment than many brokers earn. Moreover, he is not above providing female companionship.[2]

Hank's attitude toward his own firm is characteristic of most Insiders. "The House for which you work is very important, but not for the information generated by the House. If you have good contacts, you can get the reports of other Houses as fast as you can get your own. What is important is the image of the House. You want to work for a firm that has a sound reputation; your firm's reputation helps you to make contacts.

When I call a new company and say that this is Henry Strong from——, I am much more likely to get through to a top man than if I said this is Henry Strong from 'Joe Blows Associates.' "

Though Hank is primarily interested in information, he does have certain decided preferences when it comes to stocks. Hank Strong likes 'growth' stocks. More accurately, he likes a stock with a story. It is these types of stock in which Hank invests his own money. He feels that the ideal company is one which has a solid financial base and something "coming down the line", a company which can stimulate some interest and thereby develop institutional sponsorship. In his day-to-day operations he keeps an especially sharp ear open for this type of story. When he gets such a story, however, he is more likely to invest for himself than pass on the information. He explains this by noting that his institutional accounts are not interested in a company unless it already has significant institutional support. He could also find himself in a very touchy situation if it was discovered that he was pushing a stock which he had just bought himself.

Despite his various reservations about the market, Hank Strong likes the market and has been quite successful. He has developed numerous contacts during the last years and he knows how to use them. His very success causes him some difficulties. His style puts him in constant jeopardy of getting involved in potentially illegal situations. As a result, he plays down his own view of the market and his own behavior. Though he told me many times that inside information was his game, he will not admit this in front of strangers. I knew about his style from other sources before I ever met him. When I first asked him, however, about his use of inside information, he looked at me with what could only be called a shocked expression and said that if he did that he would end up in jail. He often introduced this theme after he had told me how he did use inside information, or at least information that was not commonly known.

This fear limits Hank's ability to spread the gospel of the

Insider. In contrast to Bill Chester, who is constantly preaching the Fundamentalist's credo, Hank seldom preaches. He functions more like an Eastern guru than a Western priest. He will "teach" only those who have passed through various tests; he must know them and he must trust them. Furthermore, he does not seek out converts. They must come to him. And they come. Hank Strong is continually questioned by people who want to know what he knows. In such situations, Hank generally limits himself to trading information. As he says, "My business is information, inside information. It doesn't make any sense for me to give it away for nothing."

Hank Strong's hesitancy to preach the Insider credo is not unusual for successful true believers of the Insider view. The Insider view, consequently, is not really spread by the successful. The Insider credo, or at least a variation of it, is rather promulgated by the semi- or unsuccessful. We shall meet one such character later.

Before leaving Hank Strong, one further point should be noted. Hank Strong is pessimistic about his own future in the market. He sees the market becoming more and more regulated. Already he feels cramped. This does not mean that he is about to abandon his view of the market. He firmly believes that the market of the future will be governed by supply and demand forces. Furthermore, as long as he's in the market, he's likely to remain a true believer, (a person deeply concerned with understanding how the market works in order to act). He knows that he could refocus his energies in the direction of sales. That is, he could use his information to sell stocks rather than to beat the market. This he notes, is the way most so-called "insider" types work. For better or worse, however, Hank Strong's basic concern, as with other true believers is to master the market. If and when this becomes an impossibility, Hank Strong is uncertain what he will do. He mentioned once in passing that he might become a financial writer of some sort. More likely than not, he will join the other Insiders who have turned their energies into sales.

4

A Cyclist Chartist

Bob Klein is a Cyclist-Chartist – others see him as a Cyclist Chartist and so does he. He doesn't just use and keep charts; he lives for his charts. To Bob Klein, his charts are the market. This doesn't mean that he believes anyone who can get hold of his charts will be able to understand and predict the market. His charts are his, and only he or someone with his interpretive skills can grasp what the charts say. To him the charts not only reflect the mysteries of the market, but also reflect their own mysteries.

Bob Klein is in his mid-thirties and has been a registered representative for a comparatively short time: four years. For close to ten years he was an accountant. Even now, he looks more like the stereotype of an accountant than a stockbroker. He tends to wear modestly priced three-piece suits, but he seldom wears his jacket. Usually he has a pencil stuck behind his ear and his glasses always seem to be falling off. He tends to run rather than to walk. He always seems to be carrying sheets of papers filled with numbers and charts.

Bob has followed the market since he was thirteen. He has been in love with the market for nearly all of this time. Even when he was an accountant, he spent hours every week following the market. Presently, the market, except for his family, is nearly his whole life. He arrives at his desk between eight and eight fifteen in the morning and stays to five or six in the afternoon. He spends between three and four hours going over his charts in the evening; much of his weekend is also spent with his charts. He can talk about the market for hours and never seem bored.

This passion for the market is derived from his firm conviction that the market, or more accurately, individual stocks exhibit definable activity patterns; patterns which, through hard work and study, can be grasped. To grasp these patterns is not only Bob Klein's vocation, but his avocation.

To Bob Klein, the market has a life of its own. He admits that the market is affected by economic factors and buying and selling pressures; he insists, however, that it's much more than this. The market, as a result of its own rhythms, has the ability to counteract and modify economic factors and buying and selling pressures. The market even has the ability to redefine economic information and to control buying and selling pressures.[1] To understand what the market will do consequently, it is necessary to understand the market itself. This is what Bob Klein attempts to do.

He asserts that the market is usually at least six months ahead of the economy. Where the Fundamentalist sees this as due to the market's ability to predict future economic developments, Bob Klein gives greater weight to the market's ability to determine future economic conditions. Similarly, while he realizes that the movement of the market is determined by buying and selling pressures, he sees these pressures as themselves determined by the movement of the market. It makes more sense to him, consequently, to focus on the market patterns than on economic factors or buying and selling pressures.

He is quick to add that, "The market is not easily understood. It demands a particular form of expertise. This expertise is not acquired easily. Each stock has its own particular rhythm. Furthermore, these rhythms are themselves difficult to fathom. Stock movements can be misleading; in fact, it is characteristic of stocks to mislead. One must know what to look for and what to ignore. It is almost as if each stock had a logic and spirit of its own. As a result, only those with the ability and willingness to work can hope to be successful."

Bob Klein's view regarding the basic complexities of the market, determines his general style and outlook. To Klein, nearly all customers, his own included, have no understanding of the market. Moreover, they have little chance for gaining such understanding. "Most customers simply don't have the time, interest, nor ability to become knowledgeable. The more they think they know, the less they actually know. It's, furthermore, less than useless to try to educate them. The job of the registered representative is to make them money, not to educate. The more they know, or think they know, the more trouble they are." In this regard, Bob Klein finds physicians to be the worst group to deal with. (I might just note, however, that this is a widely held opinion among market professionals.)

Bob Klein's view of his fellow registered representatives is not much different from his view of customers. "They're ignorant and don't know what they are doing. Most registered representatives are no more than order takers. They relay to their customers what they hear; they have no more idea about what the market is going to do than their customers. They swamp their customers with company reports, stories, market jargon, etc. and hope to do a little business. More often than not, they believe in what they are saying when they say it, but if the market goes against them, they will have a new story the next day. Furthermore, most registered representatives are lazy and do not do their homework." He has a similarly negative opinion about most analysts.

What then does Bob Klein look for in the market? On what does he base his charts? In the jargon of the street, he uses "technical information". More specifically, his charts are drawn in terms of the actual movement of stocks, the volume in which they trade, ratios of volume on advances versus volume of declines, support levels, ratio of up-ticks to down-ticks, etc. He also keeps data on the relationships between individual companies and various market indices. He is also interested in "odd-lot" figures, short ratios, etc. How he actually combines all this information is Bob Klein's secret.

Bob Klein's view of himself as a market expert, coupled with his present position – a moderately successful broker in a fairly large office – generates certain tensions. Whereas, Bill Chester and Hank Strong are basically content with what they are doing, Bob Klein would like to change his role. At the present time he mainly services small accounts. He feels this greatly limits him. Not only does it limit the amount of money he can make, it also restricts his visibility as a true market expert. He would very much like to be in a position to handle large sums of money where he could prove his own theories. He wouldn't do things differently, but he would get the recognition that he feels he deserves.

Where Bill Chester acts in response to economic factors and Hank Strong acts in response to "stories and inside information", Bob Klein acts in response to the market itself. This forces him to be a seller more than do the styles of Bill Chester and Hank Strong. When Bill Chester and Hank Strong buy, they are willing to wait; in fact, they expect to wait since in one case, Bill Chester, the purchase is based on the assumption that a value is being overlooked, whereas in the case of Hank Strong, the information is private. Bill Chester and Hank Strong realize that they may make mistakes, but it is only over a period of time that such mistakes become obvious. Even then they are never sure that tomorrow they won't be proven right. Bob Klein's situation is very different; if he isn't proven right, he's proven wrong, because he buys only when the market tells him that a stock is going to go up. If it doesn't go up, he read his charts incorrectly. In addition, Bob Klein's more technical approach tends to give him clearer sell signals than do the approaches of Bill Chester and Hank Strong. (Hank Strong sometimes gets a clear sell signal – word that there is a major sell order about to be executed. Such sell signals, however, are not nearly as common as are the technical sell signals for Bob Klein.)

Because the Cyclist-Chartist approach favors neither buying

nor selling, Bob Klein is more a trader than Bill Chester or even Hank Strong. Bill Chester and Hank Strong will sell, but only in response to information with long-term implications. Bill Chester is looking for long-term economic trends; Hank Strong follows big money which likewise is long-term orientated. Bob Klein follows the market itself which, by its nature, exhibits short-term fluctuations. It is not that Bob Klein's charts don't tell him about long-term trends, it's just that they are better at telling him about short-term trends. Moreover, it's difficult for him to ignore those short-term signals regardless of what he sees as the long-term trend, especially when theoretically he should be able to buy back in when the stock is ready to resume its upward move.

Bob Klein justifies his trading primarily in terms of his concept of market risk. Whereas Bill Chester and Hank Strong see market risk in terms of the amount of money their customers can afford to lose, Bob Klein sees risk inherent in every investment. There will always be opportunities to make money as far as Klein is concerned; the problem is to minimize trading losses. He admits that his approach tends to generate more commissions than other approaches, but claims that this is not why he trades. If his charts favored a long-term approach, he would work long-term. It is Bob Klein's view that the problem with most Chartists is that they try to go long term when their charts just don't provide them with the type of information which makes this possible.

One of the most interesting characteristics of Bob Klein and other Cyclist-Chartists is their attitude toward their own fallibility. On the one hand, they tend to be highly arrogant; they know what is going on and others do not. On the other hand, when they make a mistake they are much more apt to accept the responsibility for the mistake.

Bill Chester and other Fundamentalists tend to blame their mistakes on the stupidity or greed of others; "They just don't know a good buy when they see it," or "They are driving that stock out of sight and it isn't worth anything." Hank Strong is more likely to see it in terms of "the breaks of the game". Bob

Klein, in contrast, is likely to say, "I made a mistake. I should have given more weight to the advance/decline rations," or "I went too soon; it really hadn't tested the bottom," or "Those two tests were in hindsight really a single test." This is not surprising, since if he isn't wrong, (if the mistake was not his) then the charts must be wrong and if they are wrong, then he has nothing.[2]

This need to perfect his charts forces Bob Klein to work and rework his charts to make them conform to what happens. Each wrong prediction requires going back and discovering where he made the wrong interpretation. Bob Klein doesn't resent the demands put upon him by his approach. He knows that few other brokers work as hard as he does, but in his own words, "I find working on my charts to be more fun than TV."

Bob Klein's "arrogance" is offset not only by his willingness to accept responsibility for his own mistakes, but by a general wariness of the market itself. While he is critical of most customers and registered representatives, he does not ignore the trends that these people generate. Where Bill Chester tries to ignore the general psychological tide of the market, Bob Klein tries to go with the tide as does Hank Strong. Both Bob Klein and Hank Strong respond to public reports in a similar way. Where Bill Chester tends to be "above" most such reports, Bob Klein, like Hank Strong, is interested in judging their impact. If they seem to be having an impact, you go with them. Whereas Hank Strong is likely to pre-judge the impact of a report based upon who put it out, Bob Klein will wait till he sees the report's impact on the market itself. In both cases, however, there is a willingness to go along. As Bob Klein continually says, "You can't fight the tape. The tape tells you not only what the market has done and is doing, but what it will do." He doesn't care if people are buying and selling the "wrong" stocks, only that they are buying and selling. In this respect, his attitude is just the reverse of Bill Chester's and Hank Strong's. He doesn't care about anything until it has had an effect.

Bob Klein's approach would seem well suited for shorting stocks. When questioned about his, he indicated a degree of uneasiness. Theoretically, he agrees; as a matter of historical fact, however, he has had some difficulty in shorting, though he told me he had started to short some recently and thought that he would be doing more short selling in the future. Here, I questioned him about the possibilities of buying stocks making new highs and shorting them when they made new lows, this being a chartist/technical mode which some non-chartists use. Klein felt that this was not a sound chartist principle since new highs and new lows by definition mean that the stock is moving into unfamilar grounds. He personally would much rather trade stocks within known boundaries. Again, it seemed to be a case of following past patterns of the market rather than attempting to predict new future patterns.

Given Bob Klein's confidence in his own ability to read the market, I was somewhat surprised to discover that he did relatively little trading for himself. His answer, however, made fairly good sense, at least from his perspective. He stressed that he had to be objective. "I can't fall in love with any particular company. If I owned a stock, it would impair my objectivity. I would be looking for signs that it would go up. Furthermore, if I traded my own account, I would have more difficulties with some of my customers. They go along with me as long as they are making money, but they balk as soon as they are forced to take a loss. If it was known that I did a lot of trading for myself, some customers might become suspicious."

Many customers are suspicious of their brokers. It is considered a professional hazard. Such suspicions are more dangerous to Bob Klein than they are to many other brokers because Bob Klein's approach often requires that he act immediately. A stock might drop into a buy range and then move out of it again in a matter of minutes. If he can buy the stock in the proper range, he can limit his potential loss; on the other hand, if he has to chase the stock, the risk becomes to great. Consequently, Bob Klein must be able to make a phone call and get an okay in a matter of minutes. If his customers are dubious of his recommendation for any reason, the probabilities are that there will be no transaction.

Though Bob Klein relies primarily on the phone for soliciting buy and sell orders, he also makes use of the mail and personal contact, especially when things are slow. He doesn't use the mail or personal contact so much to solicit orders, however, as to solicit accounts; he doesn't focus on specific stocks, but upon his own expertise. He attempts to present himself as the "expert", not as a friend who happens to be a broker. The market itself is his love and he makes no bones about it. He would like to have you along as a customer; he can use the commissions. If it is a choice between your views and his expertise, however, your views are going to come in second best.

This doesn't mean that he won't execute any order that you give him; he will. It is just that if all you want is someone to execute your orders, then you really don't need Bob Klein. Furthermore, while Bob Klein can use your commission, he is more interested in proving his expertise which he cannot do if you don't follow him. In fact, one gets the clear impression that Bob Klein would be happier if the market wasn't corrupted by all those people trying to make money.

This attitude, coupled with his strong desire to prove himself, often makes Bob Klein feel like a duck out of water. This he is quick to admit, though he is not sure whether he would prefer to run a fund or some large accounts on his own, or whether he would be happier working as a technical analyst for someone else. I have no doubt that at the first opportunity he will do one or the other. I would not be surprised if he left the market completely for some sort of academic position.

In this regard, Bob Klein is similar to most other true believers in the Cyclist-Chartist credo. Probably less than twenty-five per cent function as brokers. I have presented Bob Klein as a broker because a broker was responsible for most of the statements attributed to him.

Though Bob Klein has been described as a Cyclist-Chartist, he is clearly more a Chartist than a Cyclist. There is nevertheless a strong Cyclist quality to his view of the market. Bob Klein uses his charts as technical tools but he sees them as much more; he truly believes that there are underlying patterns to the market. His charts work only insofar as they accurately grasp these underlying patterns. Bob Klein clearly does not see himself as merely a technician, neither does he characterize his approach as a technical approach. Most purely technically oriented analysts see themselves as trying to impose some order on a basically disordered universe (that is, the market); in this regard, they have more in common with traders, who will be discussed shortly, than with Cyclist-Chartists. Bob Klein sees himself as trying to discover a very real order which underlies the market.

The belief that there is an underlying, or transcendent order to the market is more characteristic of what may be called the universal Cyclist-Chartists. Here we confront a most unique group. What distinguishes them from analysts like Bob Klein is their concern for non-market, and even non-economic, factors which influence market cycles. These persons are interested not only in inherent patterns of the market, but such things as seasonal patterns, moon cycles, etc. which they see affecting the market.

The reasons they present in support of their views depend upon which non-market cycles they use. Those who emphasize moon cycles tend to talk about underlying biological-psychological forces; those who stress historical rhythms tend to talk about general economic-political forces. In all cases, however, they see market cycles as reflecting other, more "basic" cycles.

Though such persons exist, their numbers are few. I mention them because even more than the Bob Kleins, they deeply believe in an underlying order which is the essential element in the Cyclist-Chartist world view. They also deserve mention, because, though there are not many of them, they do have an impact upon the general mind of the market. Even persons who think that such views of the market are nonsense, tend to incorporate elements of these views. We have, for example, such notions as "summer rallies", the idea that January will reflect the movement of the market for the whole year, etc. In some cases, it can be argued that there are political/economic factors at work, but more often than not such patterns are accepted as having a force of their own. In addition, I should just add that while there are few who truly believe in such patterns, they control much more money than one might guess. I know of at least three funds which are controlled, at least in part, by such true believers.

5

A Trader

John Holland is one of the few super-professionals of the market – he is a successful trader. To John Holland the market is a game; a very serious game, but a game nevertheless. He often talks of the market as if it were a reflection of the game of life. As such, he sees it as incorporating all of the elements which are of a concern to Bill Chester, Hank Strong and Bob Klein. He sees the market as reflecting economic values, buying and selling pressures, and rhythms and patterns of its own. In addition, he gives great weight to the role of chance. All of these things are combined to generate what he calls the 'feel' of the market. To master it requires intellect, intuition and hard work. On the other hand, the market offers rewards, both financial and psychological, which can be obtained nowhere else.

Listening to him talk about the market, you might conclude that John has had an interest for it, if not a love, since he was young. Such is not the case; to all intents and purposes, John Holland fell into the market by accident. As a young man he had no knowledge of the market. The financial pages were those pages between the sports section and the funnies. Neither he nor anyone in his family ever owned any stocks. After graduating from college with high honors, he earned a Masters in History, spent some time in the armed service, worked for the government, and travelled. He was first exposed to the market during this period by a wealthy acquaintance who suggested that he buy a few shares of a company which the acquaintance thought was due for a substantial rise. John bought them and made some money. He re-invested his profits and began to follow the market. He began to read books on the market and to develop his own orientation. He found that he really enjoyed the market and that he had a good natural feel for it. He became a broker, a very successful broker.

You would be unlikely to recognize John's success on first meeting with him – he does not project the aura of wealth and influence which one immediately senses from a Bill Chester or a Hank Strong. There is a "casualness" about John Holland which can be very misleading. He dresses well but not in an obviously expensive or flashy style; he speaks clearly and with some authority, but he's not overwhelming. There is an impish quality about him.

This impish quality is directly related to John's view that the whole market is one big game. It is an important game because you play it with real money but the game is more important than the money. This was clearly revealed to me once, when he pulled a jumble of bills from his pocket. He noticed me looking at him and laughed. "You can see from the way I carry my money, that I'm not overly concerned with money per se. To operate the way I do, you can't be."

John Holland realized almost from the beginning that if he had any special ability vis-à-vis the market it was his "feel" for it. Others had better and more information but he was better able to interpret such information and to apply it. He could do this because he was more tuned into the emotive, psychological mood of the market. By tuning into this mood, he found that the information of others took on new meanings for him, meanings which seemed to allow him to make better use of the information than those from whom he received the information. He found that the market did not respond to all earning reports in the same way. Some reports were ignored; others were not. Similarly, the market responded differently to different types of stories. There were even differences in the way different stocks responded technically. In all of these cases, he found that the best guide to what the market would do was what the market was doing.

John Holland gave me some example as to what he meant by "feel for the market". "Take earnings. You always want to buy a company with good earnings, but more important than the earnings in and of themselves, is the growth in earnings. Two companies may be earning a dollar, but if one company has been earning a dollar for years and it looks like that is what they will be earning for years to come, the market will price its stock differently from a company which last year earned seventy-five cents and the year before that fifty cents, but may earn a dollar-fifty next year. It is not earnings themselves that matter so much as earnings plus price-earning ratios. Even then there are differences between companies. Some companies are able to catch the imagination of the street; others are not."

"The same is true for buying and selling pressures. With some stocks it really doesn't matter that a big fund is buying or selling; it doesn't change the picture. There are other stocks where an institutional buy or sell changes everything. Similarly, there is some buying which can be the kiss of death to a stock. On the other hand, information that some institution is unloading a large block may be bullish since the stock may have been depressed because everyone knew there was a large block overhanging it. You have to have a feel for what is going on."

"I feel the same way towards most technical information. The trouble with most Chartists and other technicians is that they take themselves and their indicators too seriously. Sometimes a stock will make a new high or a new low and it doesn't mean anything. A recommendation may just have come out which nudged it out of its normal trading range. Or a stock may be affected by a big order from some fund. At other times, you can almost see the buying coming in. You have to learn to go with the tape; you can't fight it. That doesn't mean you try to catch every swing, you would go bankrupt doing that. It is hard to explain, but if you pay attention, you get a feel for what's going on."

While John Holland relies mainly on his intuition, he is constantly educating his intuition. He spends nearly as much time studying the market as Bob Klein does. Where Bob Klein spends most of his time with his charts, John Holland is into everything. He reads the same reports that Bill Chester reads, like Hank Strong, he follows the activity of large institutions and keeps a constant eye on a range of technical indicators. In addition, he spends a good deal of time simply thinking about the market, the economy and the world as a whole. He is constantly trying to get the pulse of the market; he wants to know what the market is responding to and why.

To a large extent, John Holland tries to combine the best elements of Bill Chester's, Hank Strong's and Bob Klein's approaches. There are drawbacks to this. John Holland's approach, by its very nature, is highly complex. As a result, he faces the constant danger of being overwhelmed by information. To avoid this danger, he seeks to simplify the information which he acquires. He must remind himself everyday of what's important and what's unimportant. In doing this, he again relies upon his own feel for the market. This does not mean that he has no general rules; he has, but each rule must be interpreted in the context of the market as it is at that moment.

John Holland is, if anything, a stronger advocate of the short loss theory than Bob Klein. Where Bob Klein will let his charts tell him when he must take a small loss, John Holland will make use of a variety of indicators. He may sell a stock at a loss which is actually going up in price if he feels that its action is not good compared with the rest of the market. In contrast, he may ride a stock down through a support level, if he feels that the stock's bad performance can be accounted for by the action of the market as a whole. He is also more likely to buy a stock making a new high than is Bob Klein. One of John Holland's market aphorisms is "Buy high, sell higher."[1]

John's willingness to buy high priced stocks is in direct contrast to Bill Chester's philosophy which could be summed up by the more familiar aphorism "buy low, sell high."[2] John Holland is not only willing to pay high for a stock (from a historical point of view), but would actually prefer to. He wants to be with the market leaders. He argues that the market leaders – stocks trading in volume and making new highs – almost always out-perform the market as a whole. As a result, he has historically favored glamor stocks with high multiples. It isn't that he is uninterested in earnings, only that he feels that the market has decreed that stocks with earning growth are entitled to a higher multiple than stocks with limited growth. "Ideally," he says "what you want to find is a stock which is experiencing such growth in earnings for the first time. If you can find such a stock, you will not only get the move based on the growth in earnings but a play on the change in multiple assigned to the stock." This does not mean that he is wed to glamor stocks. If market leadership is taken over by cyclical companies, John Holland will be buying cyclicals.

In many ways, John Holland is a skeptic. He seeks out company statements on earnings, etc., but he never accepts the conclusions of the statement without reading all the footnotes. He is interested in knowing who is recommending what and who is buying what, but he seldom joins the bandwagon. He is more likely, in fact, to sell a stock if he hears that it is being recommended and to buy a stock if he hears it is being dumped. This is most likely if the recommended stock is behaving poorly and the stock being dumped is giving ground slowly. He reasons that once the buying pressure resulting from the recommendation dries up, the stock is likely to go down, whereas once the selling pressure eases, the stock is likely to go up. In short, he is constantly interpreting information in terms of the way the market itself acts.

There are many registered representatives who mouth the same philosophy of the market as John Holland. Containing as it does elements from a number of different approaches, this is not surprising. Most of these other brokers, however, are not true traders. They don't act in accordance with their "philosophy". John Holland does, and moreover has done so successfully. Starting with relatively no capital, he has amassed a significant portfolio. He has also acquired a number of large accounts. While admitting that in the earlier days he often traded with an eye to his commissions, he seldom, if ever, does so today. To begin with he doesn't need money. Today, he buys and sells exclusively to make money through capital gains. He not only feels that he can make more money this way; he also needs the constant exposure to the market to keep his feel for the market.

John Holland is not only willing, but eager to test himself and his philosophy against the market. It is this characteristic more than anything else which distinguishes John Holland and other true believers. All true believers think that they are right and expect in the long run to be proven right. Some, like Bob Klein, are also interested in testing some theory. John Holland puts himself to the test.

This need to test himself affects what John Holland does. Given his present financial situation, it makes little sense for him to trade on a short-term basis. Nevertheless, he still trades, though admittedly less than when he was younger. Similarly, he is still willing to invest substantial sums of money. Again, it's a question of maintaining his feel for the market. If he were to trade only in small sums, he would not be able to experience the tensions and doubts from which he develops his feel for the market. If he felt he could no longer do this, he would seriously consider getting out of the market.

John Holland knows that he's good. Not only does his portfolio speak for itself, but his professional colleagues shower him with respect and admiration. There is always someone wanting to know how he feels about this or that. As a result, he has managed to develop a network of very good contacts. Even Hank Strong would be pleased to have some of John's contacts. Holland not only knows that he is good, but that he is a lot better than most other brokers. Though he freely admits this, he's not as down on other brokers as are Bill Chester or Bob Klein. There are some of whom he is very critical; such feelings are generally reserved for those who he feels take advantage of their customers. The simple ignorance of most brokers he accepts more as a fact of life than as a flaw in their character.

John Holland's attitude towards his customers is similar to his attitude towards brokers. Some of his customers, he feels, have no understanding of the market whatsoever. Others have a degree of sophistication, most of which they have gained from him. Few, if any of them, he feels could survive on their own. When one of his customers begins to "second guess" him he likes to let them go on their own for a while just to teach them a lesson. Usually they fall into line fairly quickly.

Initially, like most young brokers, John Holland had to solicit accounts. For a number of years, this hasn't been necessary. Most of his new accounts, like those of Bill Chester, come in through referrals. Unlike Bill Chester, however, John Holland is likely to drop an account that causes him trouble. This is usually done in such a way that the customer doesn't know what is happening. He is allowed to act more and more on his own and then allowed to drift off. The customer more often than not, thinks that he left John Holland.

Being a trader who relies on his feel for the market, John requires a relatively high degree of discretion in what he does. Few, if any, of his accounts are officially discretionary accounts, but he handles most accounts as if they were discretionary accounts. He doesn't buy anything out of the blue for a client. He normally limits his purchases to the customer's cash reserve. Similarly, he is likely to give the customer a phone call within minutes of the transaction. There has usually also been some sort of preliminary discussion about the transaction before it occurred. He has, however, little use for lengthy discussions before such execution. He similarly makes little use of the mail.

While John Holland doesn't respect the sophistication of most of his clients, he does respect their basic attitudes toward the market. He doesn't treat all of his clients the same way. Some customers can afford and are willing to take a high degree of risk; others cannot. He takes this into account in managing his various accounts. He admits to being more comfortable with customers who can afford and are willing to trade, but he will not try to trade someone whom he feels should not be trading.

As Bill Chester needs his reports, Hank Strong his information, and Bob Klein his charts, John Holland needs the tape. He can operate without it, but it wouldn't be the same. He also needs a firm that can give him good executions. Getting an order to the floor in three minutes rather than five minutes can be the difference between making money and losing money. For this reason, John, unlike most brokers, takes a real interest in what's happening on the floor of the various Exchanges. He takes time regularly to meet and talk to the floor brokers from his firm. He similarly watches carefully the styles of the different specialists. As a result, he can almost tell you if a specialist is taking in shorts just by reading the tape. He isn't always right, but he is right more often than not.

To understand John Holland, it's necessary to remember that he enjoys the market. Bill Chester and Hank Strong are comfortable and at home in the market, while Bob Klein is addicted to it. John Holland delights in it. Simply put, he finds the market to be fun. He loves the sport of it and last, but not least, he loves winning.

To a large extent, John's enjoyment is due to his own success. There is clearly more to it than this. Having thought about it for some time, I have reached the conclusion that it's the 'game aspect' of the market which turns on John Holland and others like him. Nearly everyone in the market is, to some degree, affected by this quality of the market, but their attitude is not that of John Holland. They enjoy the excitement and action, but they don't relish in it. John Holland gets a kick out of the fickleness of the market even when he gets hurt by it. He loves to see how it twists and turns, starts and stops. He's constantly seeking to learn from it; not merely so that he can be a better trader, but also for a better understanding of life in general. Here I may be pushing things somewhat, but it is a fact that John Holland is always using market analogies to explain a wide range of non-market behavior. This is true of all true believers, but it has a special intensity with John Holland.

So what makes John Holland tick? We saw that Bill Chester is primarily concerned with underlying economic factors, that Hank Strong is primarily interested in information and market muscle, and that Bob Klein is primarily concerned with the underlying patterns – or the hand of God. What is John Holland really concerned with; what does he focus upon? The best answer, I can offer, is that he's concerned with the life blood of the market, its essential energy. One could almost say that he's interested in the market's libido. Given the way he loves and enjoys the market, such a conception is not as extravagant as it may initially appear.

While all true believers are convinced that their view of the market is the correct view; all are equally convinced that their views are bound to remain minority views. In the beginning, I found this somewhat strange. Later, it began to make sense to me; furthermore, it shed a new light upon the true believers of the market.

The true believers could be called the priests of the market insofar as they are spokesmen for the major market "religions". The market, however, is a very secular place. True believers consequently are more likely to see themselves as prophets than priests; like the prophets of old, they see themselves as living among "pagans." Without the pagans, they would not be true believers.

Are all true believers either Fundamentalists, Insiders, Cyclist-Chartists or Traders? Are there no other types? Can the types be mixed?

Probably the most central of these questions is the last since it directly bears on the first two. To some extent, the various types could be mixed. In fact, we saw that Bill Chester, Hank Strong, Bob Klein and John Holland all exhibited some sympathy for certain aspects of each other's views. On the other hand, they really do not incorporate these aspects into their own views. It would seem that one can't do this and still maintain the ideological purity required of true believers. A salesman, yes; a true believer, no. The ideological tensions seem to be too great. I ran into a number of people with their own peculiar view of the market, but I did not discover another view which had the scope or was as consistant as the four views presented above.

This is really not surprising, since, as indicated earlier, these four overviews reflect the four basic intentional dimensions which we use in defining any and all social situations. If we had discovered another basic overview, we would seriously have to question our assumptions regarding the intentional dimensions.

Though true believers tend to be loyal to a single view – whatever the view might be, these overviews become intertwined in the public domain. This creates an ironic situation, namely, that more makes for less. More concretely, though each overview seeks to impose some sort of order and sensibility upon the market – and in fact does so quite nicely – each becomes a source of added confusion when it is joined with another overview because each defines the market differently. Even when true believers of differing orientations agree with each other, (for example on buying or selling a specific stock) they normally do so for completely different reasons.

For any ture believer such ambiguities and conflicts are of little or no importance. A true believer has his own vision of the market and is seldom bothered or concerned with the views of persons with whom he or she doesn't agree. It is rather the non-believers who suffer from these contradictions; it is the non-believer who tries to navigate his way between and among the different overviews. One might ask why they even bother. The answer as indicated earlier is that they have no choice. Even persons who feel and claim that they are not interested in the theoretical concerns of the true believers are caught in the definitions of the market they put forth. How they manage to extricate themselves, is a problem to which we shall now turn.

PART III:

The Salesmen of the Market

6

The Hard Facts of Market Life

Most market professionals are not true believers; they do not have the aptitude or the inclination. More importantly, they can not afford to be, because though they often feign to be students of the market, they are first and foremost salesmen; their job is to sell stocks. That is the way they make their living.[1] This is a fact of market life. It is inherent in the very structure of the market.

Brokers are paid on a commission basis. For every sale they make – transaction they execute – they are paid a fee. The fee is derived from the commission paid by their customers; the actual fee varies from broker to broker. Some receive twenty-five per cent of the gross commission while others earn up to fifty per cent. This is true even of those brokers who are apparently salaried. In such cases the broker may have to wait till bonus time before his account is straightened out. Admittedly, it does not always work out exactly, but all brokers realize that what they take home is directly determined by the commissions they generate.

To a lesser degree, the same holds true for analysts and money managers, though their earnings may be determined more by the sums they manage than by the amount of business they are able to generate. Since a number of people usually work on a large institutional account, it is also more difficult to determine who deserves credit for any specific order; this is especially the case with analysts. Nevertheless, the general relationship holds. Sales generate income.

Brokerage firms earn their income through commissions, interest from cash in customer's accounts, and interest on margin debt.[2] This is how the market works. There are some who function on a fee basis, but even then the management fee is often determined by the number of transactions that the account is likely to require though it will offically be set in terms of sums under management. In many cases, there is a management fee plus a transaction cost agreement. Whatever the specific arrangement, everyone knows that the greater the number of transactions, the greater the income. They similarly know that the more business generated, the greater the rewards to the individual broker or money manager.

It is not surprising, therefore, that most market professionals see their job primarily as soliciting and executing market orders. This situation puts most brokers in a difficult position. On the one hand, they are supposed to give expert advice to their customers; and on the other, they have to generate business. For those who have the ability to give expert advice, this situation does not create great difficulty. Market expertise is one of the best sales tools that a broker has;[3] most brokers, unfortunately, do not possess it. In fact what expertise they have more often than not serves to make them cautious rather than aggressive. It is easier to recognize the dangers inherent in an investment than to pick a stock which is likely to double. As a consequence, whatever expertise the average broker has may actually hinder him or her from aggressively soliciting orders.

Most brokers know this. While all brokers consider themselves to be market professionals, few consider themselves to be market experts; among those few, fewer are in fact experts. Most will freely admit that they are not stock analysts; they are salesmen. Their job is to sell stocks. They try, of course, to sell stocks which will appreciate in value. If the stocks they recommend do well, it is easier to make future sales. The solicitation of orders is the main objective, however, not picking market winners.

A broker is more than a salesman. One can't simply walk into a Wall Street firm and expect to be able to function as a broker; the market is governed by a wide range of rules and regulations.[4] There are numerous types of orders, held and not-held orders, etc. There are also options, short sales, "box" sales, etc. A broker has to know how to execute all of these orders; he has to know what forms to fill out and how to fill them out. He, furthermore, has to know what releases are required from his customers and the types of securities which are required in each situation. In short, a broker has to be a fairly sophisticated functionary.

In some firms, there is the added pressure to move specific stocks. This is more likely in firms which do a lot of underwriting, i.e., they acquire large blocks of stocks for dispersion to their customers. It is generally the small producers who are most exposed to such pressures, though a number of substantial producers also engage in this type of operation.

Most customers are aware of these pressures. If anything, they overestimate their importance. In contrast, market professionals tend to down play them. Many will go so far as to deny them. They cannot deny that it is specifically in terms of these factors that the market defines itself. Every year a list of the ten 'best' brokers is compiled. What is the criterion used in establishing this list? Those brokers who best predicted what the market would do? Those brokers who picked the most outstanding stocks during the last year? Those brokers who made the most money for their clients? Those brokers who best outperformed the market as a whole? Those brokers judged by their colleagues to understand the market best? Those brokers judged by their customers to be the most considerate and helpful? The answer is no to all of these questions. The "best broker" list is determined by the amount of commission business generated.[5]

Within firms another process is at work. While the so-called best brokers are clearly those who produce, a modest producer who goes by the book, and whose orders are always in the proper form, will generally be judged a "good" broker. In contrast, a modest producer who continually makes bureaucratic mistakes, whatever his market expertise, is likely to be out on the street. Such a broker is too dangerous to keep around. He can expose a firm to all sorts of suits and sanctions.

This explains why so few brokers, money managers, or even analysts become true believers. There is simply no profit in it. It would be wrong to conclude that the average broker, money manager and analyst has no interest in the views of the true believer. Whatever their personal understanding or lack of understanding and whatever their personal bias towards theoretical models in general, no market professional can ignore the general overviews of the market since their customers and their clients expect them to have an integrated overview of the market. Whether they like it or not, therefore, they are forced to simulate some sort of ideological commitment.

Most, especially the retail broker, will simulate whatever beliefs work best in soliciting orders. They will make use of whatever ideology or credo seems most appropriate at the time. Sometimes they will focus upon earnings and other sorts of economic fundamentals; at other times, they will stress a story or some sort of "inside" information; at other times, they will refer to technical factors and yet at other times, they will rely upon their own feel for the market. The particular mix will be influenced by the firm for which they work, the biases of their customers, where the market is at the time, their most recent experiences, who they talk to, etc.

It may appear as if all, or most, brokers are phonies. Such a judgment is really not fair. The average broker who behaves in this way more often than not is fully convinced about what he is saying when he says it. Few deliberately try to mislead. Their problem is that they have no strong opinion as to what's going on or what makes the market work. They listen to what others have to say and are convinced by this argument or that in much the same way as their customers. More often than not, it's a simple case of the blind leading the blind.

There are other factors which influence the particular stance that a broker, money manager, or analyst will take at any time. Nearly all brokerage firms provide their salesmen with recommendations. Besides pushing specific stocks, these recommendations usually push one view of the market. Most firms' recommendations rely heavily on economic factors; some make use of technical factors. Customers also vary in the types of companies they want to own. Some want to maximize safety, while others want to maximize capital gains. Given the salesmen's prime concern with sales, he normally goes with what he has.

There are good reasons for going along with one's firm or one's customers. In both cases there is protection if the stock doesn't work out. In the case of firm recommendation, the broker can always fall back on the follow-up "explanations" that the firm will no doubt put out. In the second case, he can always remind his customer that it was his (the customer's) choice, as well as his own. Obviously, in neither case, is the customer likely to be happy, but neither is he likely to see the broker as the sole villain.

While going along with the opinion of others affords some protection from abuse, it also makes it more difficult to acquire true expertise. You become a follower not a leader. You are too concerned with the views of others, which are themselves often inconsistent, to develop your own view. This doesn't necessarily mean that such brokers cannot do a reasonable job for their customers. It does mean that they are dependent upon the sophistication of their firm and/or their customers. In this respect, the salesman broker is quite different from the true believers, who lead rather than follow.

Some salesmen – those who work for the larger firms with a great deal of in-house research – can operate almost exclusively in this passive manner; most cannot. Even the best firms make "bad" recommendations and even the most sophisticated customers can react irrationally. Most brokers, if they are to survive, must develop some sort of discrimination, though it will be different from the discrimination required of true believers. The true believer forces himself to stay with those stocks which conform to his own view of the market; he is concerned with picking stocks which he believes will outperform the market. The salesman has another concern; he must be able to pick stocks that his customers can live with.

These two types of discrimination are not unrelated. If a salesman feels that a particular stock will not work out, he is not likely to recommend it. On the other hand, most brokers live in dread of knocking a stock and thereby thwarting a sale only to see the stock double. The difficulty is to know when a stock should not be recommended regardless of its future action.

What would constitute such a situation? When the broker is likely to find himself out on a limb. This is apt to happen when a customer is tempted to buy a stock unlike those he normally buys or when the firm is recommending a company unlike those it normally recommends. In such situations, if things go wrong, the customer is likely to accuse the broker of putting him into a bad situation, while if it was a firm recommendation, there may be no follow-up "explanation". To avoid such situations, a good salesman must understand his customer and how his firm operates. He must know when a customer is following a mere whim and when his firm is pushing a stock. This requires more psychological and political expertise than market expertise.

Even those who attempt to survive by psyching out their customers and playing firm politics, must know the rhetoric of the market. They don't have to become true believers, but they must be able to project such an image, even if it is a very eclectic image. Whatever other talents he might have, he cannot hope to generate customers confidence nor to become part of the market establishment without such an image. For most brokers, this is not a difficult task since they acquire the rhetoric and credos of the market by osmosis.

Salesmen, almost by definition, are not wedded to one

approach. They can and do change their "line". Such a change may be due to a switch in firms, exposure to a new service, securing a new contact, or acquiring some new accounts. It may be due to no more than some hard times with his old approach. Despite such constant changes, most salesmen at any one time favor one approach over the others. It simply creates less strain.

A broker could come up with his own reasons for buying a particular stock at a particular time. He could use astrological signs, his mother's intuition, the market symbol of the company, etc., but it is doubtful that his customers would accept such reasons. It is also doubtful that any reputable firm would allow him to make such recommendations for any length of time. Brokerage firms prefer their salesman to rely on orthodox reasonings which means, at least in form, the reasoning of true believers. This is a fact of market life to which even the most opportunist salesman must adjust.

Other factors constrain salesmen to favor one or another of the general views of the market. There is an affinity among the different sale approaches and the different overviews of the market. This was alluded to above when it was noted that most firm recommendations tend to have a Fundamentalist bias. To understand how and why this is so, requires a few words of clarification.

In analyzing true believers, each type was shown to conceive of the market in a different way. Fundamentalists see the market in basically economic terms; Insiders, in interpersonal terms (who is buying, who is selling); Cyclist-Chartists, in terms of some sort of underlying or transcendent order; and Traders, in terms of the "life forces" of the market itself. An analogous process characterizes the way most salesmen look at sales. Some see sales primarily in economic terms; their task is to provide an economically attractive product. Others see sales primarily in interpersonal terms; their task is to convince customers to make purchases. Others see sales as part of an ongoing orderly process; their task is to match buyers and sellers. Others see sales primarily in what I can only call libidinal terms; their task is to satisfy specific emotive needs.

Where these biases determine the way true believers look at the market, they determine the way salesmen look upon the sales relationship. The economically orientated salesman sees himself primarily as a salesman for a specific product which, in most cases, is provided by his firm. The interpersonally orientated salesman sees himself primarily in terms of his various customer-broker relationships. The ordered market salesman sees himself primarily in terms of the market as a whole, whereas the libidinally orientated salesman sees himself as a trained guide for the adventuresome.

Given that salesmen's biases for their firm, customers, the market as a whole, and market "action" are influenced by the same conceptual bents which influence the way true believers look at the market, it is not surprising that each type of salesman tends to prefer the orientation of the true believer most like himself.[6] A salesman's primary concern, however, is sales. A Firm Salesman, consequently, is at best a pseudo-Fundamentalist; a Customer Salesman, a pseudo-Insider; a Market Salesman, a pseudo-Cyclist-Chartist; and an Action Salesman, a pseudo-Trader. With these points in mind, it is time that we take a closer look at these salesmen of the market.

7

The Firm Salesman: A Pseudo-Fundamentalist

The most common type of retail broker is the Firm Salesman. It is not difficult to figure out why. All brokers are paid to sell stocks; it doesn't matter if they are selling stocks to customers or selling the stocks of customers. The end results are the same. It is not easy to sell stocks; a stock has to be packaged like any other merchandise. As the Madison Avenue saying goes, people buy the sizzle not the steak.

True believers like to do their own packaging, that is they provide their own reasons for buying or selling a particular stock at a particular time. Most brokers have neither the ability nor the interest to do this. They have to get their packaging material from someone else. Most make use of the packaging material provided by their firm. It is readily available; there is always plenty of it and whatever its limitations, it usually looks good.

Firm recommendations are also relatively safe. If the stock doesn't work out, the broker can be assured that in most cases his firm will provide him with a reasonable explanation of what went wrong. Furthermore, since other brokers will have been recommending the same stock, neither the broker nor his customers will have to suffer alone. While this does not negate the pain which accompanies market losses, it does tend to assuage it a little for nowhere does the aphorism 'Misery loves company' hold truer than in the market.

By using firm recommendations a broker can cultivate an image of himself as a "team player". Such an image can have positive pay-off. First, it tends to sooth management; they know that you are not about to rock the boat by recommending stocks of which they disapprove, or knock the stocks they recommend. Secondly, by recommending the stocks recommended by the firms, the broker is doing his bit to prove the firm right. If the brokers working for a particular firm can generate a demand for a stock recommended by the firm, that stock is likely to do well, at least in the short run. Management knows this and has ways of showing its appreciation. This is especially the case if management is involved in underwriting.

None of the above requires that the firm itself follow a Fundamentalist line. They could push a stock for any reason they choose. Most firms, however, with sizeable in-house research favor a Fundamentalist approach. Their reasons for doing so are similar to the reasons why most brokers use firm recommendations. To begin with, by projecting a Fundamentalist image both the firm and the broker can present themselves as down to earth, no nonsense financial advisors; they are dealing with economic "reality". This tends to generate a sense of trust in both the broker and the wares he is selling. It also allows the broker to "cool out" his customers if the stock recommended does not do well since he can continue to remind his customer that the stock has "true" value regardless of what its price is at the moment.

The Fundamentalist approach also insures that the firm will always have new stocks to recommend. It is easier to have a slew of in-house analysts looking for fundamentally "undervalued" situations than to have them find companies which should be bought for other reasons, though most firms will include such other reasons if they are available. During the last few years, most firms have begun to rely more heavily on technical factors. With few exceptions, however, the heart of most recommendations remain fundamentally orientated. As a result, most Firm Salesmen can be said to favor, or at least to appear to favor, the Fundamentalist credo.

How does this all work in the broker's day-to-day operations? First, he can expect to find on his desk almost daily the latest research reports put out by his firm. These reports are worth at least a few telephone calls to customers who have in the past indicated some interest in the company or industry recommended. The more aggressive the salesman, the more calls. A synopsis of the report, usually also provided by the firm, may also be included in a general mailing to prospective customers. Such mailings are one of the most distinguishing marks of firm salesmen. The more established Firm Salesmen use them less than do the less established, but they still use them.

Firm Salesmen are not generally high pressure salesmen. They have a product to sell and they try to sell it. Because of the nature of their product they don't have to push any particular item. If the customer doesn't like one item, there will always be another. In fact, if the Firm Salesman is too aggressive, he tends to work against his own image. He is not in the business of recommending "hot" items, but in recommending sound investments. If a customer wants to think it over for a few days, it is perfectly all right. The stock will probably be just as good a value next week as it is today.

While Firm Salesmen initiate sales, they are strongest when they are on the receiving end, that is, when they are asked about a specific stock by one of their customers. In such situations, they are able to check out the stock with their research departments – the larger firms have an official position on most regularly traded stocks. By making one or two in-house calls, the broker can come back to his customer with a comprehensive evaluation of the situation. More than once I have seen such brokers receive an inquiry regarding a stock about which they knew nothing, only to have them return the call within a few minutes sounding as if they have followed it all their lives.

This last point touches on an important development of the last few years. It has been my thesis that most Firm Salesmen favor a pseudo-Fundamentalist view because this is the view emphasized by most firms. In recent years, because many firms have begun to place more emphasis upon technical analyses, Firm Salesmen have begun to make greater use of technical information. This does not contradict what was said earlier about the Fundamentalist bias of most Firm Salesmen if one remembers that they are only pseudo-Fundamentalists. When such technical information comes from a respectable firm, it is no longer simply technical information, but part of a general recommendation of an established firm. One could say that by being filtered through an established firm, technical information is transformed into fundamental information.

When one compares Firm Salesmen with true Fundamentalists, men like Bill Chester, a number of other differences emerge. The Firm Salesman is, for all practical purposes, completely dependent upon his firms's research; he seldom does any research of his own. The true Fundamentalist, in contrast, relies on his own research. Even when he likes a particular piece of research done by others, he will check it out for himself. This generates very different attitudes toward firm research.

When asked to judge the value and importance of their own firm's research, the Firm Salesman will nearly always say "very important." He is, furthermore, likely to tout highly the quality of this research. He is also likely to indicate respect for the research of other firms, though this will vary from house to house. (Brokers working for the larger firms with extensive in-house research tend to be more chauvinistic toward their own research than those working for smaller firms.) The true Fundamentalist, in contrast, is apt to be very critical of most in-house research. As far as he is concerned, most such research is written with the sole purpose of pushing some stock and is superficial at best. While he may respect some institutional research, he's quick to point out that most good research is seldom available to the average broker or his customers.

There are other differences. Where the true Fundamentalist

tends to put his people into a few stocks in which he believes, most Firm Salesmen favor more highly diversified portfolios. A true Fundamentalist will continue to acquire stock in the few companies he likes as long as they are within his buying range. The Firm Salesmen is always coming up with new situations. The true Fundamentalist is much more likely to stay with his choices over a period of time; he is apt to sell them only if they appreciate to a point where he feels they are fully valued or if there is some basic economic change. The Firm Salesman moves his people in and out of situations to insure that they have the resources to "take advantage" of the next "opportunity" his firm is likely to offer.

The way true Fundamentalists and Firm Salesmen look at and treat their customers also differ. Firm Salesmen on the surface appear to respect their customers more. They are more likely to go along with their customers' judgments than the true Fundamentalist. In part, this is because they are interested in making sales; customers are usually willing to go along with their own hunches. The true Fundamentalist seldom will go along with his customer's ideas.

This does not mean that Firm Salesmen think their customers know what they are doing. They have no more respect for their customers' market judgment than true Fundamentalists. It's just that they are not as ready to say so publicly, at least not to their customers.

There is an additional factor worth noting in this regard. Both the Firm Salesman and the true Fundamentalist are more likely to respect the opinions of their wealthier customers. In the case of the Firm Salesman, it is the customer's wealth per se which generates respect. Again and again, when asked which customers are the most sophisticated, they answer those with substantial financial resources, period. The true Fundamentalist, in contrast, is not impressed by his customers financial resources; he is impressed by the economic information such customers are likely to have. He does not listen to them for their market judgment but for the specific business information they may have.

Above, I stated that the Firm Salesman only "appears" to

respect his customers more. I stressed the notion of appearance because it can be argued that the true Fundamentalist exhibits more genuine respect. The true Fundamentalist is more aware that he is playing with other people's money. While he may respect their market judgment less, his concern for their general financial situation is greater. The true Fundamentalist is also more likely to explain his customers' lack of market sophistication in terms of the time required to understand the market than in terms of their lack of intelligence or their greed. He tends to see himself much more as a teacher and guide than do Firm Salesmen. While he is less likely to go along with the hunches of his customers, he is more likely to explain why he feels the way he does. Since the true Fundamentalist generally has more discretionary control over his accounts than do Firm Salesmen, it is more important that his (the true Fundamentalist) customers understand why he has acted as he has.

The true Fundamentalist also tends to be more of a contrarian than Firm Salesmen. Whereas, Firm Salesmen generally recommend popular stocks (stocks which are being recommended by others), the true Fundamentalist tends to favor stocks out of favor. In fact, if his firm or some other firm recommends his stock, he is more likely to become a seller rather than a buyer. In the opinion of the most true Fundamentalists, when a stock begins to get such recommendations it means the stock is already fairly valued.

Lacking true Fundamentalist's expertise, Firm Salesmen tend to be more cautious. Many hesitate to have their customers on margin. Most true Fundamentalists, in contrast, use margin freely when they think they have a solid situation, especially if the yield of the stock covers the bulk of the interest charges. The fact that the true Fundamentalist generally manages larger accounts who can afford to take bigger risks also plays a role in this regard, as does the general rule that margin accounts have assets of $5,000 or more.

The more cautious approach of the Firm Salesman is reflected in another way. Many Firm Salesmen have become sellers of covered options. During the last few years, many have begun to recommend a specific stock purchase coupled with the sale of options on the stock. Such transactions are sold as "no risk" situations, which to a large extent they are. On the other hand, they could also be called "no win" situations since the customer is not likely to benefit if the stock goes up appreciably. This is why most true Fundamentalists are negative on such transactions. They are willing to sell covered options in certain situations: The stock has not behaved very well, but he wants to maintain his position; or, he has already had a pretty good move and he is milking it for a few more points. To buy a stock and sell an option at the same time, however, makes little sense to a true Fundamentalist. If he wants to invest for a fixed return, he is much more likely to put his customers into bonds.

Perhaps the most significant difference between the true Fundamentalist and the Firm Salesman is their own involvement in the market. The true Fundamentalist nearly always follows his own advice. If he's recommending a purchase strongly, he's usually buying it for himself. Few Firm Salesmen do this. Those who do invest, generally invest in companies very different than those they recommend. They tend to play with much more speculative stocks and to rely much more on tips. A sizeable number of Firm Salesmen never invest in the market. They will generally explain their behavior by asserting that it is wrong for them to be investing their own money, since it would serve to cloud their objectivity and force them to divert too much attention to their own accounts.

There are exceptions to all of these patterns. Some invest their own money in the stocks they recommend; some recommend only a few companies. Some are more technically orientated than fundamentally orientated. They are the exception, because once a broker decides to follow the recommendations of his firm he is almost committed to the other attitudes and behaviors discussed above. In this respect, the Firm Salesman is as much constrained by his view of the market as any true believer. As we shall see, the same situation holds for the other types of salesmen.

Most Firm Salesmen are, as noted above, team players. In sociological terms we could say they tend to be organizational men. This is not true of most true believers. Admittedly, Bob Klein would like to become an analyst which would, in effect, make him more a part of the firm. It is also true that many successful true believers become partners. In all cases, however, their primary concern is to understand the market.

Firm Salesmen, in constrast, are generally more than willing to leave the market behind to take a position in management. Many of the good ones make it. They are the recruits from whose ranks officer managers and senior sales personnel are drawn. From the firm's point of view, this makes eminently good sense. An office manager doesn't have to be a master of the market. His job is to keep a number of registered representatives in line. He has to know what is expected by the firm and how to insure that others conform to these expectations. The good Firm Salesman is ideally suited for this role.

It also helps if he is a good producer. It is difficult for someone to push a specific approach if it hasn't worked for him. As a result, it often happens that the more successful Firm Salesmen are Firm Salesmen for a relatively short period. This has implications for the average investor to which we shall return. First, we will look at some of the other types of salesmen who frequent the market.

8

The Customer Salesman: A Pseudo-Insider

The Customer Salesman best fits the common sterotype of a stockbroker. One or two can be found in nearly any brokerage office; moreover, they are quite visible since they tend to be outgoing and talkative. They are full of ideas and usually on the go both literally and figuratively. Furthermore, they tend to be among the more successful salesmen. They are also the most difficult brokers to pin down conceptually. The reason for this is quite simple: a Customer Salesman will tell you what you want to hear. This requires its own skill. A successful Customer Salesman must be a good social psychologist.

Where the Firm Salesman focuses on his product – the stocks being recommended by his firm – the Customer Salesman focuses on his customers. He wants to know the degree of risk they're willing to take, the types of companies they like, how much capital they have to invest, the types of stories they like, and their tax situation.

In order to get this information, the Customer Salesman tries to stay in close contact with his customers. He encourages them to call him regularly, even if they're not about to make a specific trade. If he doesn't hear from them for a period of time, he will call them even if it is only to say hello. He'll also try where possible, to initiate frequent meetings. In fact, he will attempt to make it a personal relationship rather than a strictly business one.

Such an approach does not work with all customers. The customer must have a fairly strong interest in the market; he must enjoy talking about it in general terms. A customer who is only interested in buying stocks that will appreciate in value, is more likely to be put off by such attention than impressed by it. The customer must also have a degree of market sophistication, or at least believe he does, for without such sophistication, much of what his broker will be telling him will be meaningless.

This last point bears on the similarities and differences among Customer Salesmen and true Insiders. Like the Insider, the Customer Salesman is interested in information as to who is buying and who is selling. He is not interested in this information for its intrinsic value, but because it reflects the dynamics of the market which interest his customers. The ideal customer for a Customer Salesman is someone who wants to be part of the market. He wants to know what is going on.

This was aptly revealed by a Customer Salesman describing one of his best clients. The customer was semi-retired. He had built up a very successful candy business. He felt, however, that life was passing him by. He was the owner of a substantial business; he made a good living; he felt he was bright and interesting, but when he went out socially, he had nothing to talk about. The market had changed all of this for him. Because of the market, or more correctly his relationship with this particular broker, he had become a star attraction. Whatever the market news, he had something to add to the conversation.

It takes a good deal of time to provide such services. Most Firm Salesmen, with their numerous small accounts, couldn't provide such service even if they wanted to. Customer Salesmen can because, for the most part, their customers, in their desire to be part of the market, trade more. Their assets may be no greater than those of the customers of the Firm Salesman, but they generate substantially more commissions.

By focusing upon the desires and interests of his customers, the Customer Salesman provides a cushion for himself similar to that provided to the Firm Salesman who goes along with the recommendations of his firm. When things go wrong, the Customer Salesman can usually point out to his customer that it was as much his decision to buy a particular stock as it was the broker's. This is seldom the case, but most Customer Salesmen are able to convince their customers that it is.

The Customer Salesman's approach, however, is more dangerous. Once a firm makes a recommendation, they cannot deny they did so; they can come out with a new report hedging their original report, but the original report is still public information. Customers can, and often do, deny that they ever had any enthusiasm for a particular situation, especially if it goes sour.

While there is always a risk of a customer turning in this way, the risk is greatest when the salesman uses a customer's hunch. Most customers are more willing to admit that they had agreed with the broker (that the situation sounded good given his information) than to admit that their instincts were wrong. On the other hand, it is usually easier to make a sale when a customer has a hunch. A successful Customer Salesman has to walk this narrow line. In any given situation, his decision is influenced by what he knows of the customer. He approaches customers with a history of "turning" more warily than those who take reverses in stride.

To minimize the risk of customers turning, many Customer Salesmen attempt to convince their customers that they are sophisticated investors. Even when knocking a customer's suggestion, they're supportive. They're likely to point out the merits of the suggestion even while they're rejecting it. Such supportive treatment serves not only to keep the customers happy, but also to provide a foundation for the sharing of responsibility.

What are the Customer Salesmens' true feelings about their customers? Like most market professionals, they have a fairly low opinion of lay investors. Their reasons for belittling lay investors, however, differ from those of the Firm Salesmen. Firm Salesmen criticize their customers' lack of understanding and laziness. Customer Salesmen emphasize their arrogance and greed. Every Customer Salesman has a story about a customer who pushed him into doing one thing only to turn around and blame him later. They seem to have an equal number of stories about customers who had to be pushed into a situation, who then took the credit for themselves when the stock did well. To a large extent, Customer Salesmen create these problems since they feed into their customers' images of themselves as astute investors. Most brokers know this and admit it; they still get very upset when they have to deal with such situations.

Though Customer Salesmen are critical of lay investors in general, they have a slightly higher opinion of their own customers or, at least, some of them. Many have a number of relatively sophisticated accounts. It is only the more experienced investors who feel comfortable with such brokers; the Customer Salesman approach is not likely to work with investors who know very little about the market. Even the most arrogant person has some idea of his or her limitations.

Most Customer Salesmen need to believe that some of their customers know what they are doing since they require sources of information and their customers constitute an important source of such information. Most rely primarily upon professional sources, but the more sources the better. Nearly every Customer Salesman I have met has one or two accounts whose opinion they respect. Such customers are usually other market professionals, ex-brokers, or persons with good business connections. There is also the fact that Customer Salesmen are very personable as a rule and simply come to like their own customers.

Most Customer Salesmen have little or no respect for their firm's research; many comment that it's junk. This is especially true of those who work for the smaller Wall Street firms. Moreover, most don't seem to care. On the other hand, they value highly the reputation of the firm itself. This makes sense because a firm with a good reputation, which is financially sound and which has a good back office, gives customers a sense of confidence. Here again, the important thing is maintaining good customer relations.

While Customer Salesmen tend to be negative on the research put out by their own firms, they are likely to praise the research of other firms. Initially, this may seem to be a simple case of some firms having better research than others, but it is not. Customer Salesmen speak more highly of the research done by others, regardless of the firm for which they work. On second thought, this makes perfectly good sense. The Customer Salesmen is in the business of relaying information. Reports put out by his own firm don't qualify as information; they are firm recommendations. Reports that he is able to acquire from other firms do constitute information. Moreover, the customer is able to get such information only through his broker. As a result, another firm's reports serve to strengthen the tie between broker and customer, whereas recommendations from one's own firm put the firm between the broker and customer.

Stressing, as he does, his own relationship with his own customers, a successful Customer Salesman is often approached by other firms. For most firms such "headhunting" is good business. It is not just that such brokers generate a lot of business and hence firm income, but that they are in a position to take most of their clientele with them. This generally is not the case with even the most successful Firm Salesmen. The Firm Salesman's customers have been buying the firm's product not the salesman's product.

Though most successful Customer Salesmen are temperamentally not organizational men, many do accept management positions. In nearly all cases, however, they insist upon maintaining their own accounts. Where the successful Firm Salesman, who moves into management, often cuts back on his own accounts to focus attention upon organizational problems, the customer broker who moves into management is more likely to serve as a model for other brokers. Rather than checking up on his fellow brokers, he is expected to help them improve their own sales techniques. In some cases, even this is not expected; he is rather given a management position and the added income which comes with such positions simply to keep him within the firm.

In light of the great similarities between Customer Salesmen and true Insiders, one might ask what the differences are. It is a question of priorities and basic goals. The true Insider is interested in collecting information in order to understand what is happening in order to master the market. The Customer Salesman is interested in selling stocks. The true Insider is not interested in just any story or any piece of information: he's very selective. He is not likely to give much weight to what his customers have to say. Neither is he interested in information bearing on institutional activities if he feels such information has already been discounted. The Customer Salesman will make use of any and all information which he feels could effect a sale. He is as likely to make use of economic information (earnings projections), and technical information (chartist reports), as information dealing with who is buying and who is selling.

Where the true Insider tries to restrict himself to "first-hand" information, the Customer Salesman is perfectly happy to use secondary and tertiary information. This is not to imply that a good Customer Salesman will use any information he gets his hands on. They know that you can have too much of a good thing; they also know that if they put their customers into too many bad situations, they will suffer in the long run. Given a choice, they would rather put their clients into situations which will work out. The most important thing, however, for most Customer Salesmen is that the information "sound good".

Earlier it was noted that Firm Salesmen require reports on more companies than do true Fundamentalists. The same can be said for Customer Salesmen vis-à-vis true Insiders. The true Insider, like the true Fundamentalist, is content to find those few situations which he feels will work out. A Customer

Salesman can't survive with a few situations. His customers differ and he must have situations for all of them. This is why he must rely on secondary and tertiary sources of information. He can not afford to put in the time that a true Insider does following up on a single story. Where a true Insider like Hank Strong will visit different houses and talk to various people, the Customer Salesman must rely on information which he can glean between telephone calls with his clients.

The biggest difference, however, is the one that was mentioned earlier in our discussion of Firm Salesmen. Customer Salesmen, like Firm Salesmen are not heavily involved in the market. The reasons offered are basically the same. They feel that if they were deeply involved in the market, they could not be as objective nor could they give their accounts the attention they require. Customer Salesmen differ from Firm Salesmen, in that most have a history of personal involvement though few have been successful. Many, if not most, Customer Salesmen, in fact, became brokers by virtue of the personal contacts they established while customers themselves. Many even hoped to make their fortunes through their own investments. As they saw their commission incomes dissipate in the market, they concluded that their energies were better spent in attempting to develop a clientele rather than in trying to beat the market – they because Customer Salesmen.

There is one way in which Customer Salesmen are similar to true Insiders. Like Insiders they take a negative view towards government regulations. They are willing to admit that such regulations protect customers from unscrupulous brokers and firms, but most add that governmental interference with the free market, in the end, actually hurts their clients more than it helps them. When pushed as to what should be done to protect the small investor nearly all respond that brokers must be made to deal more honestly with their customers. With many, "honesty" seems to be an obsession. In part, no doubt, this is due to their own misgivings about the way they treat their customers. It can also be seen as highlighting once more that to the Customer Salesmen the most important thing is the customer-broker relationship.

9

The Market Salesman: A Pseudo-Cyclist-Chartist

As Firm Salesmen mirror Fundamentalists and Customer Salesmen mirror Insiders, what I have chosen to call Market Salesmen reflect the Cyclist-Chartist view. Like Cyclist-Chartists, Market Salesmen see the market as governed by its own rhythms and patterns. They differ in that (1) they are not concerned with mastering this "order" but in using it to make sales, and (2) in seeing this "order" as applying to the behavior of their customers as much if not more than to the market itself. They see themselves as order takers willing and able to provide a specific type of information.

Market Salesmen must be ready to comment on many more stocks than a Bob Klein. Bob Klein limits his customers to those stocks which he personally follows. Market Salesmen are not able to do this. They are first and foremost salesmen and as such must be able to comment on the stocks which are of interest to their customers. As a result, they cannot rely on their own charts; they simply do not have the time, nor in most cases the ability to maintain the number of charts required. They are forced, consequently, to rely upon the charts and services of others, primarily those of advisory services. Most Market Salesmen are more than willing to do this; it is easier and the charts and recommendations of such advisory services generally carry more weight with their customers than would their own.

There are non-ideological reasons in the making of most Market Salesmen. Quite simply, many brokers who adopt the Market Salesman style cannot function as Firm Salesmen or Customer Salesmen. In some cases they work for firms which do not supply them with a sufficient number of in-house recommendations. Others are just uncomfortable with the Firm Salesman approach. Few have the temperament to function as Customer Salesmen, or if they do, they have not been able to establish the contacts or the clientele that this approach requires.

While few Market Salesmen are such by choice, they would appear on the surface to be ideal brokers. In fact, their actions are most in keeping with the official job description of a broker put out by the New York Stock Exchange, i.e., to execute customer orders and to provide the backup services and advice that customers may request. Nevertheless, Market Salesmen, or order takers which is what most really are, seem to be ducks out of water, much as their true believer counterparts, the Cyclist-Chartists.

Few are able to get a firm handle on the market; many appear to be overwhelmed by it. They are no more ignorant of the ways of the market than other salesmen; their problem is that they believe there is something to know. Similarly, as indicated above, most believe that the customer-broker relationship should follow certain set patterns, but they have difficulty determining just what this relationship should be. As a result, they tend to be erratic. When they feel that they are in tune with the market, usually as a result of one of their advisory services being correct for a change, they can become very aggressive salesmen. At these times they function very much like a Bob Klein except that they use the recommendations of others. On the other hand, when they feel that they are not in tune with the market, usually as a result of their pet advisory service being wrong, they tend to become very passive. During these periods, they are likely to function merely as order takers.

Market Salesmen tend to be among the more critical denizens of Wall Street. They tend to be critical of their firm, of other firms, or other salesmen, and of most customers. In this respect, they are much like their true believer counterpart, the Cyclist-Chartist. Unlike the Cyclist-Chartist, they generally try to camouflage their true feelings, though some don't do a very good job of it. They realize that they must maintain an upbeat presentation of self if they are to generate any business. Many manage to maintain this posture by hoping that tomorrow they will be able to latch onto the 'right' service. Few expect to find an advisory service which will provide them with sure market winners; rather they hope for a service in which they can believe and which will enable them to generate sufficient business to earn a comfortable living.

Unlike the true Cyclist-Chartist, most Market Salesmen have fairly low self-esteem. In part this is due to the ribbing and criticism they receive from their co-workers and management. They receive such criticism and ribbing because (1) they are generally only marginal producers, (2) they are not good team players, and (3) as a group they lack the sociability characteristic of Customer Salesmen. In addition, most feel that their relative lack of success is due, in some measure, to their own inability to get a proper handle on the market.

Though there are considerably fewer Market Salesmen than either Firm Salesmen or Customer Salesmen, one can find a Market Salesmen or two in most brokerage firms. They will usually be among the younger salesmen trying to get established, especially in firms with limited in-house research. In firms with a great deal of in-house research, the young, aspiring broker is more likely to become a Firm Salesman. One will also find some older Market Salesmen. More often than not they will be brokers who have tried other approaches and failed. Where the young Market Salesman is likely to evolve into some other type of salesman, or even to become a true Cyclist-Chartist, the older Market Salesman is likely to find the going more and more difficult. There is clearly no place in management for him; most firms, in fact, prefer not to have them around at all. As a result, a Market Salesman's career is likely to take him from firm to firm with each new firm being slightly less prestigious than the one he just left. Many eventually find themselves with no job at all.

The Market Salesman is in most respects a weak carbon copy of the Cyclist-Chartist. In one interesting respect, however, Market Salesmen tend to reverse a pattern characteristic of Firm Salesmen and Customer Salesmen. Market Salesmen tend to play the market as much if not more than do their true believer counterparts, the Cyclist-Chartists. In part, this is because Cyclist-Chartists do not play the market much whereas Fundamentalists and Insiders do. In addition, however, Market Salesmen have a greater propensity for playing the market than Firm Salesmen and Customer Salesmen. Firm Salesmen and Customer Salesmen have few illusions about what they are doing. They will invest if they think they have found an exceptional situation, but they entertain few fantasies that one day they will become privy to some oracle. Market Salesmen tend to maintain such illusions; in a very real sense they function as their own best customers.

Many firms keep on their Market Salesmen because of the business they do in their own accounts. Few Market Salesmen are constantly in the market. The common pattern is for a Market Salesman to trade in spurts. He may be inactive for two years and then become very active for six months. At any given time, most are not active; though they express the hope that they will be able to be more active in the future. Again, it is a matter of coming up with the right formula. Firm Salesmen and Customer Salesmen, in contrast, generally say that they expect to do less trading in the future.

Despite their propensity to trade their own accounts, Market Salesmen are first and foremost salesmen. Even their own trading should be seen in light of their role as salesmen. Firm Salesmen and Customer Salesmen know what they are selling; Market Salesmen often do not. Moreover, they know that most of their customers are skeptical of the products they offer. The Market Salesman, consequently, is often put in the position of having to prove to others and himself that his products are worthwhile. He often tries to do this by trading for himself. There is the added factor that most being marginal producers grasp at any opportunity they see to make a little money.

The Market Salesman may very well be a dying breed. The consolidation of many of the smaller Wall Street firms makes it more difficult for him to survive. Such consolidations have eliminated many of the houses for which he could work and given rise to a whole new group of Firm Salesmen with whom he cannot compete. They also find more and more of their potential customers subscribing directly to the services they use. Many of these services have found it necessary to direct their appeal to lay investors because brokerage firms are generating more and more of their own in-house technical research.

Nevertheless, it would be premature to discount such Market Salesmen entirely. The very difficulties they now confront could be their salvation. It was noted above that Market Salesmen tend to function almost exclusively as order takers when things are not going well. Traditionally, this type of passive orientation has received little if any managerial encouragement. With the growth of discount houses, the prospects for Market Salesmen willing to function as order takers could change dramatically. In many ways they are ideally suited for such positions. Dealing, as is normal, with more sophisticated investors, they are not expected to make specific recommendations; on the other hand, their interest in the market as a whole and their technical orientation could well make them of great value to such sophisticated investors. Admittedly, few will be able to earn as much as a successful Firm Salesman or Customer Salesman, but they are likely to do as well if not better than most are doing now.

10

The Action Salesman: A Pseudo-Trader

Few people on Wall Street stimulate as great an emotional response as Action Salesmen. They are loved and hated, often by the same people and, sometimes, at the same time. Why? Because the Action Salesman supplies his customers with "action". He is not there to offer safe investments; most Action Salesmen are not even concerned with making you money. Rather, they're there to allow you to participate in the excitement and drama of the market; they are there to give you some 'kicks' and to allow you to vent whatever gambling instincts you might have.

It may seem as if investors hardly need anyone to help them do this, and that consequently, it requires little or no skill to be an Action Salesman. Nothing could be farther from the truth; it requires more skill to be a successful Action Salesman than any other type of salesman. The market is not all action; for every exciting situation there are a score of dull investments. The Action Salesman must know where the action is and where it is likely to be in the future. Furthermore, he must be able to move his customers in and out of situations with as little damage as possible. All of this requires a sophisticated feel for the market.

The concept of "feel" is central to an understanding of

Action Salesmen. It is also this "feel" for the market which relates the Action Salesman to his true believer counterpart, the Trader. Like Traders, Action Salesmen have an emotional relationship to the market; they are tuned in to the social-psychological dynamism of the market. In this respect, they are similar to Customer Salesmen, but whereas Customer Salesmen are primarily concerned with the psychological needs of their customers, Action Salesmen are tuned into the social-psychological mood of the market itself.

Action Salesmen, like Traders, see the market as a game. Like Traders, they are usually addicted to the tape. Unlike Traders, they're not committed to winning. Where the Trader attempts to separate himself from his emotions and to use his emotions as a guide – which more often than not means going against his emotions – the Action Salesman rides the emotional tides of the market. Unlike the Trader who attempts to master the market, the Action Salesman, in common with other types of salesmen, is primarily interested in sales. To the Action Salesman, the emotional moods of the market are not tools for understanding why the market behaves as it does, but rather tools for obtaining market orders. He is not there to get his customers to control their emotions, but rather to enable them to experience emotional exhilaration.

Most Action Salesmen project an image similar to that projected by Customer Salesmen. Like Customer Salesmen, they tend to be outgoing and gregarious; if anything, they tend to be more "flashy". They are, however, more interested in the market than with their customers. In this respect, they are like Bob Klein and John Holland, though their main concern is "Can I sell it?"

Action Salesmen are very aggressive. Timing is all important. If one wants to catch an explosive situation, one must be willing to move quickly. If one waits even a day or two, the excitement may be all over. Consequently, Action Salesmen pressure their customers to move at once when they think the time is right.

To be successful, an Action Salesman must be aware of the

likes and dislikes of his customers. Most of his customers like action or they wouldn't trade through him. On the other hand, some like and can take more action than others. A good Action Salesman must know what different customers can take, both emotionally and financially. If he tries to push a conservative customer too hard, he is likely to lose him entirely; he is just as likely to lose a "high roller" by not providing him with enough action.

Action Salesmen make use of different types of investments. Most focus upon the heavily traded glamor stocks which are more likely to give customers a ride for their money. There is the added inducement that because they do trade in volume, they are highly visible stocks. Even when they are not moving one way or another, his customers are likely to feel that they are still in the middle of things. They can follow these stocks more easily since they are normally mentioned in the market reports carried by many radio stations.[1]

The heavily traded glamor stocks have another advantage. It is easier to get in and out of them. This is important to the Action Salesman, because though he is not primarily concerned with making money for his customers, neither does he want them to be wiped out. He must be able, consequently, to get his customers out quickly if things start to go wrong. Again, this is similar to John Holland's approach. There is a difference, however. John Holland is likely to get out only when he doesn't like the way the stock is acting; the Action Salesman might have to get out because his customer can not take it any more.

While Action Salesmen like heavily traded glamor stocks, many also have an affection for their opposite – thinly traded OTC (over-the-counter) stocks. Here they are willing to give up some of the safety of heavily traded stocks, for what may be potentially even greater volatility. The situation is analogous to a preference for playing red and black at roulette or playing specific numbers. Many Action Salesmen will play both types of stocks depending upon the likes and dislikes of their customers; others stick with one type or another.

Most Action Salesmen have traded their own accounts in the past and most claim that they still like to trade for themselves. In fact, it is almost impossible for anyone to function as an Action Salesman who has not traded for himself; there is just no other way to develop a feel for the market. Most will freely admit, however, that they seldom do very well when they trade for themselves. Many even wish that they could refrain from trading completely; they often add that they would be a lot richer if they could stop. In short, Action Salesmen like Firm Salesmen and Customer Salesmen realize that the only way they are going to make any money is through the business they can generate. At one time in their lives, they may have had the hopes of becoming successful Traders like John Holland; now, most realize that the most they can hope for is to be a successful salesman.

While some Action Salesmen have adjusted to this situation gracefully, most are tinged with some bitterness. This bitterness influences their view of the market and their opinions of those involved in the market. While some are willing to admit that there are a few successful Traders, most claim that there is no such thing. The Trader who makes it big one year, in their opinion, will ninety-nine times out of a hundred lose it all the next year. Their attitudes towards Fundamentalists, Insiders, and Cyclist-Chartists are basically the same. As far as most Action Salesmen are concerned, anyone who thinks that he can beat the market is just kidding himself.

This cynicism colors their view of management, money managers and lay investors, though it takes a slightly different form in each case. They are most negative on management because they believe that management knows the market can not be beaten; they similarly have contempt for money managers who think they can beat the market. It is only the lay investor for whom they have any sympathy, because "he doesn't know any better."

Given this attitude, one might wonder why most Action Salesmen don't just quit. They don't, because beating the market is not what it is all about. They are in the market because it is exciting. Moreover, they believe that is why most investors are in the market. To put their customers into mutual funds or other more "stable" investments wouldn't serve to make their customers rich, but it would take away the one thing that the market has to offer, namely, excitement. This they are not willing to do; furthermore, they don't think that is what their customers would want them to do even if they knew the market can't be beaten.

Action Salesmen acquire a different type of clientele. In part, this is by customer choice. Many have had a number of past brokers with whom they were unsatisfied. Only when they found an Action broker did they feel that they were getting their money's worth. In part, it is due to the Action Salesmen. Most Action Salesmen are very wary of dealing with customers who are not willing, in fact eager, to trade. They are uncomfortable with the accounts of "widows and orphans". If such accounts come their way they are more than likely to direct them somewhere else. If they insist on staying with him, he's likely to put them into nonvolatile situations and forget about them.

Given their negative view of other market professionals, one might expect that Action Salesmen would be subject to the same abuse alotted to Market Salesmen. This is seldom the case because there is one major difference between the average Action Salesman and the average Market Salesman; even the average Action Salesman tends to be a good producer. First, most of his clients are fairly wealthy; second, he trades them a great deal. Whatever management might think of him, they are not about to send him on his way.

For his part, the Action Salesman is not about to go anywhere either. First of all, there is really no place for him in institutional sales. Institutions (pension funds, banks, mutual funds, etc.) are not in the market to play games: even if they wanted to, they couldn't. Government regulations, plus the institutional process of decision making, make it impossible for such institutions to trade the market the way Action Salesmen do. There is similarly no place for him in management. Admittedly, a very successful Action Salesman may be made a partner to keep him, as with a successful Customer Salesman, but he will not have any management role. Most firms already have enough managers who are market cynics. Finally, and most importantly, even if such positions were offered him, the average Action Salesman wouldn't take them, because to do so would mean leaving the market that he loves. Many wish they could leave, but most admit that they are addicted to it.

One might legitimately ask whether the Action Salesman, like the Market Salesman, is a dying breed. Like the Market Salesman, he seems to be fighting the trend. The key issue here is how successful he is. The poor and modest producers are probably a dying breed; management doesn't like the image they give Wall Street. The successful ones, however, will be around as long as there is a market. They will be around because there are people who are more interested in the excitement of the market than in making money. As long as such people exist and as long as the market can satisfy their needs, the Action Salesman will remain a part of the market.

With the Action Salesman, we complete our analysis of the four basic types of saleman, each a counterpart to a true believer. We have not yet, however, exhausted all possibilities. The fact is that there are market professionals who are neither true believers nor salesmen in the strict sense in which these categories have been defined. Their prime concern is neither to master the market nor to sell stocks though they often feign interest in both. What they are primarily interested in doing is "explaining" or, more exactly, rationalizing the market; I call them consequently the "market rationalizers".

Like true believers and salesmen, market rationalizers are constrained by the four basic overviews presented earlier. They tend, however, to be even more eclectic than salemen in the ways they use these overviews. The reason for this is quite simple: they want to be able to explain what has happened and will use whatever frame of reference seems useful. One rationalizer may rely more heavily on one overview and another on another overview, but a rationalizer will never be "true" to a single overview.

While all rationalizers attempt to explain why the market did what it did, there is a significant difference among them in their attitudes towards the market. Like most compulsive rationalizers, they all exhibit a high degree of fatalism which in some cases takes a very bitter form but in others a more detached one. The former I call the Market Cynics; the latter are generally referred to as the believers in the Efficient Market Theory. We will deal with each type in turn.

PART IV:

The Market Rationalizers

11

A Market Cynic

For Market Cynics the market has a sinister character which they are more than willing to publicize – as a result, they are an embarrassment to the market. They exist even though most market professionals wish that they did not. In fact, they constitute a fairly large group and are consequently very noticeable.

True believers seek to understand and "beat" the market; salesmen try to sell stocks. The cynics want to explain why things went wrong; but what explanations do they give? Ironically, though not surprisingly, explanations are framed in terms of the same overviews of the market used by true believers and salesmen.

One may ask why any broker would become a cynic. The answer is quite simple; most are unable to function as either a successful true believer or as a salesman. They have tried and failed, and are now primarily concerned with explaining this failure. How do they do this?

Those with a Fundamentalist bias tend to stress the irrationability of the market – their "undervalued" stocks have not gone up, because the market is crazy.

Those with an Insider bias complains about their lack of information and the conspiratorial nature of the market.

Those with a Cyclist-Chartist bias bemoan the deceptions and traps inherent in market cycles.

Those with a trader bias curse their bad luck. Most cynics, however, make use of whatever "explanation" seems appropriate at the time. If salesmen are more eclectic than true believers, cynics are the most eclectic of all.

Despite their admitted failure, cynics have a real influence on the market. In fact, they are often the clearest spokesmen for the various market philosophies though seldom in an integrated way. Investors who have lost money are generally more interested in knowing *why* than those who have made money. They want an explanation. The cynics are able to provide such explanations. Whereas the various market philosophies discussed above are implicit in what the true believers and salesmen do, they are explicitly presented by the cynics.

In order to have a better understanding of such cynics, I think that we should get to know one of them more intimately, since in many ways when you know one, you know them all. I have selected a character who has a decided bias for the Insider view of the market; he could be called, a Tipster. I have selected this particular type as he is the most common; he also best reflects the essential quality of cynics. As in the case of the true believers, I have focused upon one individual, but have camouflaged some of his personal characteristics.

Henry Geller has been in the market nearly as long as Bill Chester: about forty years. His father, with whom he never got on too well, was a successful broker, but lost much of the family's money during the 1929 crash. From the time he was young, Henry always wanted to be a broker. The family name and portfolio was still good enough in the early forties to land him a job with a small but respected house. Since then, Henry Geller has worked for four different firms; these relocations have not always occurred under the most amicable of conditions. At the time I met him, Mr Geller was with one of the larger retail firms. He was not among their best producers, though he made a reasonable living. This was reflected in his "office worker" appearance.

Henry Geller describes himself as "basically a Fundamentalist." In addition, he claims to keep his own charts and to follow a number of the chart services. He is, however, neither a true Fundamentalist nor a true Cyclist-Chartist: he is, if anything, a "tipster". In his own words, "It is not what you know in this business, it is who you know." As far as Henry Geller is concerned, his problem is that he doesn't know the right people. This attitude is reflected in almost everything Henry Geller has to say regarding the market.

Henry Geller's firm puts out numerous reports. Whereas most of his co-workers rely heavily on these reports, Henry Geller feels that they are useless. "By the time I get a chance to see one of these reports, all the big guys have already seen it and acted on it." He has no interest in these reports as sources of information; he is only interested in the final recommendation, to buy or sell. He feels this way about all such reports. He doesn't care if the house putting out the recommendation is a big house or a small house, a firm with market muscle or one with no reputation at all.

This concern for buying and selling is reflected in Henry Geller's attitude towards charts. Charts are useful, he claims, because they tell you if the stock is being bought or sold. He is consequently more interested in chart movements than in chart patterns; in this respect he differs from most Cyclist-Chartists. As he says, "When you see a lot of buying going on in a stock you know that someone knows something. You can't really know what is going on unless you are one of the big boys on the inside, but the charts can help you." This attitude towards those who know and those who don't, including himself, pervades his whole attitude towards the market. "Those guys upstairs never tell us anything unless it is too late to do anything."

Henry Geller's attitude towards those who are in the know and those who are not determines not only how he sees the market, but how he sees his customers, what he reads, to whom he talks. On the whole, Henry Geller has a very negative attitude towards customers; as far as he's concerned, less than ten per cent know what they are doing. The ten per cent who know do so because of their own contacts. It does not matter how successful they are, but who they know. One of his best customers, Henry Geller told me, is a guy who doesn't trade much, but his brother is a president of a big bank and he gets all sorts of good information. "My barber is also a good contact, because he hears all sorts of things from his customers who include some of the biggest guys on the street."

It is consistent with Henry Geller's view regarding inside information that he does not see, or even look for, general market trends. "You have to stick with the companies with the story regardless of what the market is doing." When asked how he can separate the good story from the bad story, he answered, "It's the guys with money who know what's going on." Here he added that "You have to be very careful, because when you make money, your customer will take the credit, but if he loses any money, it is your (the broker's) fault." On this point, most brokers agree, but few seem to feel the injustice of it all as strongly as Henry Geller.

While Henry Geller sees the road to riches paved with good information, by which he means private information, he sees his own survival as being based upon his ability to generate confidence among his own customers. This he tries to do by maintaining personal contact, especially with his larger accounts. As far as he's concerned, mail is useless except for bringing in a few new accounts. "People don't want to read about a company; they want to know if they can make some money. The phone is okay, but really you have to go out and see them."

Henry Geller sees most of his customers as not only ignorant, but greedy. While he condemns this greed, he claims he adjusts to it. "I'd prefer to buy blue chip companies, but with my customers I have to buy second line companies. They like them because you can get better moves out of them since they trade in less volume. Smaller companies respond better to stories and rumors than do large companies."

Similarly, while asserting the virtues of holding stocks for long-term gains, he claims that most of his customers want to take their profits. He admits that he often supports this approach because it generates more business. "Why should I fight them; it's their money," and adds "There is also constant pressure from upstairs to move stocks. You've got to do some business everyday around here if you want to be kept."

Henry Geller dismisses the normal sources of information – "By the time the information is public, it is of little use" – and in much the same way, although he talks about good buying and bad buying, he doesn't follow most of the more popular indicators of such buying. He was unfamiliar, for example, with the "odd lot" figures. His answer, when questioned about the use of the odd-lot figures was quite characteristic of him. "That's good information, but I can't get a hold of them." (They are published daily in both *The New York Times* and *The Wall Street Journal,* two papers he claims to read everyday.) In all of these respects, he differs from Hank Strong who, in addition to relying on his "inside" information, makes extensive use of public sources.

Though Henry Geller's market philosophies serve primarily to justify his own lack of success, it would be misleading to interpret his view of the market purely as an example of "sour grapes". It is as much due to his sense of 'Henry Geller against the world.' Even on those rare occasions when he is riding high, he sees the world as out to get him.

Henry Geller does not care what the value of a company is providing someone with substantial financial resources is willing to buy it. Similarly, he doesn't want to hold on to a company no matter how underpriced if someone with a large position in the stock is selling. This does not mean that Henry Geller feels that economic factors are irrelevant; it will be remembered that he claims to be a Fundamentalist, of sorts. What it does mean is that he feels that most published economic information is of questionable veracity. He is fond of pointing out how a company can juggle its books to either hide earnings or to increase earnings. In short, the economic facts are not facts until they have been verified by people in the know. The way these people verify such facts is by buying and selling. The earnings picture on a company might be bad, but if a big mutual fund is buying, then they must know something. Similarly, the future for another company might look good, but if the president is selling, he does not want to wait until the bad news becomes public.

When questioned about the soundness of this approach, given the relatively bad record of mutual funds, insiders, trust departments, etc., Mr Geller merely smiled. Again, it was clearly a question of not believing the public information. "I don't believe any of that stuff. That's why I'm a contrarian." (A person who prefers to go against the dominant market trend.) "The big boys often use market moods for their own advantage. When they are trying to buy they like to put out pessimistic predictions, and when they are trying to sell, they like to put out optimistic predictions." Having watched Henry Geller over a period of time, however, I would say that he goes with the tide more than against it.

To Henry Geller, the market is a battle; one's opponents are the other investors. One's success is determined by one's resources. Ideally, the best resource is money. To quote; "Someone with enough money can make the market do what he wants." For the little guy with little money, it is necessary to know what the guys with the money are doing. This requires both guile and caution. Caution requires that one never expose oneself to the manipulative powers of the big boys. In line with this reasoning, Henry Geller avoids short selling and margin. "Half the time they let you short a stock, they are only setting you up to run the stock on you. They suck you in on margin, then they drop the stock on you."

Given Henry Geller's attitude toward the stock market, one might wonder why he remains a broker. He has no choice; at least he doesn't feel he has. The market is all he has ever known. In addition, the combat aspect of the market fascinates him. He loves the fight though his own nose often gets bloodied. Deep down he feels that with a few breaks he can be a winner. All that he needs is a few new customers with good contacts or a few good stories. "That is all you need because once you get a hold of some good information, you can start trading it with the other guys. Then you are made."

If Henry Geller appears to be a fairly sad character, it is because he is. In part, this is due to his lack of success; in greater part, it is due to his cynical, almost "paranoid" view of the market and life in general. Most people in the market have one or two stories about "inside" information, but few see the market as controlled and governed by such information. Given Henry Geller's market record, he either has to feel paranoiac or he would have to change his view of the market.

Henry Geller receives a good deal of flack from his fellow brokers, for always talking about the way the big boys are taking advantage of the little investor. Such an opinion doesn't help to generate business for most retail brokers. It doesn't even help Henry Geller since he puts off as many customers with this line as he gets with his own so-called inside information. Why then does he do it? Because Henry Geller is convinced that the market is one giant conspiracy. Moreover, this vision of the market is more important to him than selling stocks.

One might expect that the Henry Gellers would have little effect upon the way other people perceive the market. He is not held in much esteem by his fellow brokers or by his firm's managers. He is, however, a spokesman for a number of small investors. Moreover, there are times when he influences the thinking of other professionals; generally when these other professionals have experienced a particularly serious unexpected reverse. At such times, Henry Geller's view of the market can be quite consoling.

* * *

It may initially seem strange that the views of a person who is a notorious failure should ever prove to be consoling, but upon analysis it is anything but strange. Henry Geller's views are often consoling because he always has an answer-after the fact. He always has an answer after the fact, because he doesn't try to have an answer before the fact, or more accurately, he has a built in escape clause, namely that the market is "rigged." In short, Henry Geller does not really care what the market is going to do, but is only interested in coming to terms with what it has already done. That is why he can be consoling and also why he is doomed to failure.

Is it possible, however, to share Henry Geller's view of the market as somehow "unbeatable" without accepting his paranoia? The answer is "Yes". An example of a broker with this view is Dave Gibbons, a believer in the Efficient Market Theory of the stock market.

12

A Believer in the Efficient Market Theory

Dave Gibbons has been a retail broker, an institutional broker and an analyst: at present he is a money manager. He is employed by the trust department of a relatively small bank; he is in charge of two substantial pension funds and a number of smaller private accounts. He earns a very good salary, is pleasant and quite polished. In many ways, he comes across as a younger—he is in his early forties—less established, Bill Chester.

This is not surprising since he claims that he was a young Bill Chester for a number of years in that he shared Bill Chester's view of the market. Entering the market with a masters in economics, he found the Fundamentalist-Economic view most congenial, but became disenchanted with it in the mid-sixties. Here he was buying sound companies for himself and his customers while all the "go-go boys" were making all the money. He soon became convinced that there was more to the market than fundamentals. He admits that the fact that he was unable to make a living as a Fundamentalist played a role in his conversion.

He is quick to add that it was more than these financial pressures that changed his mind. Functioning as a broker, he developed more and more respect for the technical side of the market. He never adopted the extreme views of a Bob Klein, but he became convinced that there was something to be said for a more technical approach. He similarly developed more respect for the influence of information, though again never to the extent of a Hank Strong or a Henry Geller.

In discussing this period of his career, he characterizes himself as a junior version of John Holland. For a while he was quite successful; he began to think he was a pretty good trader. He focused upon growth companies, followed the tape closely, and traded freely. Then he took a couple of beatings. When this happened, like a good Trader, he stepped back to get his bearings. He tried again and got hurt again. After that, he says he came to the hard conclusion that he really wasn't meant to be a Trader. It was not that he thought he couldn't do it if he tried – the period during which he got hurt was an especially difficult period – but rather that he just was not enjoying it. He wasn't sleeping and his stomach was constantly upset. "It takes a special type of person to trade in the market. I'm just not that type."

When pressed on the matter, he expressed the opinion that there are only a few people who, for a combination of reasons, can trade successfully over the long haul. Consequently, it is not a sensible approach for most, including himself.

As a result of these various experiences, Dave Gibbons concluded that there is no way for most people to beat the market. This does not mean that he believes people should not be in the market. To quote: "A significant proportion of assets belong in the market; stocks are still the best protection against inflation. Moreover, stocks are bound to move higher as the economy grows. You can not beat the market, however, because the market at any time is the best indicator of its own true value. You can't beat the market because it responds too quickly to all significant information. By the time you hear or see anything, be it information on earnings, the decision of a large fund, a technical breakout, etc., the market has already discounted it." To use the market jargon of today, Dave

Gibbons became a convert to the Efficient Market theory of the market.[1]

The conclusion put Dave Gibbons in an awkward position. Here he was, a self-proclaimed market expert who believed that he couldn't beat the market. He soon found out that he wasn't alone. True, not many brokers or money managers felt this way, or at least were willing to admit it publicly, but there was a sizeable number of people with substantial sums of money who did. Among his own accounts, he found two persons who had reached the same conclusion. Whatever reservations he had were finally put to rest with the emergence from the academic world of the Efficient Market theory of the market.

Dave Gibbons has constructed what could be called a semi-index fund; that is, his investments are, by and large, a mirror image of the market as a whole. He has not gone so far as to invest a little bit of money in every company; he does not think it is necessary nor does he have the resources. He tends rather to stick with major companies. He tries, however, to avoid weighting his investment in any direction. He doesn't want to beat the market; he just doesn't want to be beaten by it. The only real flexibility he allows himself is the amount of money he has in the market. He always maintains fifty per cent in the market and thirty per cent in the equivalent of treasuries; the other twenty per cent can be either in stocks or treasuries depending on his general feel for the market as a whole.

As a convert to the Efficient Market theory, Dave Gibbons has had to keep a low profile. The bank for which he works does not favor the Efficient Market theory, and their official line is that they can beat the market. Some of his clients also still want to beat the market. Fortunately he works for a fairly conservative bank and his clients tend to be conservative. He is able, therefore, to justify his investments in terms of diversification for safety. Nevertheless, he believes that most of the people with whom he comes into contact know what he's doing, and since he has done pretty well during the last few years, especially in contrast to most other money managers, they haven't pressed him. Moreover, he believes that in the future his view of the market will become more respectable among market professionals.

Dave Gibbons' opinion of almost everyone associated with the market is influenced by his view of the market. He is not as down on the small investor, for example, as are most market professionals. He agrees with other professionals that the small investor can not beat the market, but in this respect, he judges the small investor to be no different than anyone else. He is irked only by the small investor who is greedy or who expects to make an easy fortune in the market.

It is the professionals who really bother him, because as far as Dave Gibbons is concerned, they should know better. It is this notion that distinguishes Dave Gibbons' low opinion of his fellow professionals from the general low opinion that we have seen most professionals have of each other. They claim that most professionals are out for themselves, and are lazy. They may also complain that they don't understand the market, but this is usually a secondary complaint. Few expect to be students of the market. It is specifically this lack of understanding which most upsets Dave Gibbons. "There simply isn't that much to understand. The problem isn't that they don't understand the economics of the market, the importance of information, market cycles or the dynamics of the market, but rather that they will not admit that they can't beat the market." This, of course, is the same attitude expressed by Ben Decker and to some extent Jack Reed.

While most market professionals take a dim view of the Efficient Market theory, it has a seductive quality. If failing to outperform the market is not the fault of the broker, analyst or money manager, he can't really be held responsible. There is something very reassuring about this. As a consequence, even among those who most vociferously attack the view, there are a good number who secretly fancy it.

Dave Gibbons could be considered a type of true believer; he has a clear market philosophy. He differs from the others in that his belief does not serve as a basis for action. True believers, by definition, believe in order to act; Dave Gibbons' understanding of the market has put him in the peculiar position of not being able to act. His understanding has taken on a life of its own; he is more interested in explaining the market than mastering it.

Though Dave Gibbons and other believers in the Efficient Market theory believe that one cannot beat the market, few of them are likely to spread the gospel. Most of them have too much to lose. It is rather the investors themselves, especially the big ones, who are likely to become converts. Many have not done as well as the market averages over the last few years. Despite this fact, they have spent considerable sums in commissions and management fees. To many, the Efficient Market theory is very attractive. It would seem to dictate that they need only invest their funds in a diversified portfolio; there would be no more need to trade or incur the expenses associated with trading.

Dave Gibbons is fully aware of this possibility. Nevertheless, he believes there will always be a need for people like himself. In fact, if more people became converts to the Efficient Market credo, he is likely to do very well. A number of others might suffer, but given his expertise in setting up such portfolios, he doubts that he would. Moreover, he's not that concerned even if his own job does become obsolete. He feels, with his background and experience, that he could always find a job with some business school. He wouldn't earn what he now earns, but with the assets he has accumulated, he thinks he would be all right.[2]

The Efficient Market theory may not be right, but it is simple and there is something very attractive about a simple theory. In light of this fact, I asked Dave what would happen if it ever really took hold. Wouldn't that create conditions which would negate its own validity? If everyone put their money in an index fund, wouldn't the market cease to adapt to new information? (This question has been put to me by a leading Wall Street analyst in our discussion of the Efficient Market theory.) After hesitating for a moment, he answered that it probably would. "If that happened, we would have a whole new ball game." Dave Gibbons is not about to lose much sleep over this possibility, however, because he does not believe that the Efficient Market theory will ever be more than a minority view.

This study has so far focused on: (1) the ambiguity of the market and the source of this ambiguity (the market's interpretive character); (2) the four basic market overviews (the Fundamentalist/Economic, Insider/Influence, Cyclist/Chartist and the Trader/Market Action), and (3) the various ways these overviews are used by true believers, salesmen and rationalizers. Despite these changes in focus our main concern has remained "the mind of the market"; that is, our main objective has been to examine the various ways the market is seen, defined, and interpreted. Unfortunately in pursuing this path it has been necessary to gloss over a number of related issues of some importance in order to pursue our prime objective. More specifically, in order to introduce the various types as directly as possible, I have deliberately said very little about the overall mix of the various types, background factors of the various types, and the shifts and changes among types. It is time that we gave some attention to these questions. Once we have done that we will be in a better position to grasp the mind of the market as a whole.

PART V:

Putting It All Together

13

The Types through Time

Though we have described in detail the various market types, we have said little about where they come from or what is apt to happen to them. The reason for this is that the market styles of most market professionals are likely to change over time; this makes it very difficult, if not impossible, to get a permanent fix on the various types at any given moment or to make detailed generalizations regarding the overall mix of types which will hold at all times. This raises a number of important questions. It would seem to imply, for example, that background characteristics have a relatively minor impact in molding market philosophy. As is so often the case, the truth of the matter is considerably more complex; it is not so much that background factors are irrelevant as it is that they play only a contributing role. Most market professionals are minimally middle class both in their class of origin and their present class. Over eighty per cent of brokers, for example, are college graduates and over fifty per cent have been involved in the market before becoming brokers.[1] Moreover, whatever differences there may be regarding their views of the market itself, they are a relatively homogeneous group in terms of their more general political-economic-social philosophies. Background factors, including social class, are consequently at best of secondary importance when it comes to explaining why one person sees the market different from another.

What factors then are relevant? Here I can only make certain tentative generalizations based upon my own data in combination with that put out by the New York Stock Exchange.[2] To be specific. Three factors seem to favor a Fundamentalistic/Economic orientation: a business orientated educational background; a history of family involvement in the market; and substantial capital of one's own. The main factor favoring an Insider/Influence view of the market is a sales background; an accounting background seems to be most significant in supporting a Cyclyst/Chartist view of the market, whereas a history of being a "player" of some sorts seems to be correlated with the Trader/Market Action view.

It could be argued that these factors are, in fact, class related. Having substantial capital and a family with a history of market involvement, for example, would seem to imply fairly high social class. On the other hand, a history of being a "player" might indicate lower social class origins as might a background in accounting. A history in sales meanwhile, especially if it were a family business of some sort, might indicate something in between. While there is some truth to such generalizations, my own data does not support them in any significant way; there are so many different variables associated with each case that it is impossible to make any firm judgments.

However important one's general orientation may be, it does not in and of itself determine one's market style and/or philosophy. There is still the very important question of whether you are a true believer, salesman, or rationalizer. Here background factors are clearly much less significant than one's own experiences in the market, especially the degree of personal investment success. The actual impact of investment success and/or failure, however, differs from type to type.

With those who favor the Trader/Market Action orientation, success generally produces a true believer, whereas failure is likely to produce an Action Salesman; persons with Trader/Market Action leanings seldom become rationalizers. First they tend not to go in for "rational" explanations; secondly, they tend to be too positively disposed to the market to adopt the inherently neutral to negative view of the market implicit in the rationalizer's stance.

Success also strengthens the true believer inclinations of those with a Fundamentalistic/Economic point of view. If it can be shown that the economic return is greater in some sort of sales or research capacity, however, most persons with a Fundamentalist orientation are likely to become salesmen or analysts. Those with limited personal success meanwhile are likely to become salesmen—Firm Salesmen if possible—whereas those who have done very badly are apt to become rationalizers, especially if they lack the support of a good firm.

Personal success can serve to strengthen the true believer leanings of those with an Insider/Influence view and those with a Cyclist/Chartist view. It can also have a quite different impact. Success in establishing contacts may serve to make the role of Customer Salesman more seductive and lucrative to those than with an Insider/political view of the market than that of true believer. For those with a Cyclist/ordered bias, such success may make the role of highly paid rationalizer more attractive than the role of true believer, especially if their own charts indicate that it is extremely difficult to outsmart the market. Personal failure in both cases is likely to produce a rationalizer of the cynic variety, though this is most likely to be the case with those who have an Insider/political view of the market. This is, in fact, what seems to have happened to Henry Geller.

There are other factors which influence the specific market style of any given individual. There is the firm he or she works for and even more importantly the people with whom he or she actually comes into contact, especially during the first months as a professional. A particular book or even article can also have a decided influence over the reader's entire market philosophy. Most important, however, is the fact that the market itself changes over time and as a consequence exerts different influences upon market participants.[3]

At the risk of overstating the case, a highly depressed market favors a Fundamentalistic perspective; a young bull market favors the Insider; a middle bull market favors a Trader perspective; and a mature bull market favors the Cyclist/Chartist. A real bear market favors no perspective though the Market Action and Cyclist/Chartist views should theoretically lend themselves as easily to bear markets as bull markets since both should allow one to short the market.

The reason for this seems to be as follows: in a highly depressed market there are by definition many fundamentally undervalued situations; it is relatively easy, consequently, to buy stocks – or sell them if you are a broker – for sound fundamentalist reasons. In an early bull market meanwhile, it is often easiest to buy on information. It is generally a time for reinvestment of institutional funds; it is also a time when many companies enter the market on behalf of their own shares. Historically it has also been a time of takeovers. In short, it is a time when the "big boys" often begin to flex their muscles and when consequently information on what they are doing often proves rewarding. In contrast, it is specifically in the middle of a bull market when fairly major fluctuations begin to characterize the market that the Trader comes into his own. The Cyclist/Chartist meanwhile usually likes to wait till the "trend" has been established. No one really likes a bear market because all market views are aimed primarily at making money in up markets. Bear markets consequently don't serve to strengthen one particular orientation over another so much as they serve to strengthen the rationalizer stance in general.

By this point it should not be surprising to anyone that the market projects an image of ambiguity. Not only have we discovered four different market philosophies, each of which lends itself to three distinct uses, we have also found that these various types themselves are likely to change over time.[4] There is still the question, however, of whether we have exhausted all possibilities. Though we have examined a good number of different types, it would seem that we have also skipped over numerous others.

What about, for example, the option broker, the OTC

broker, the "go-go" broker, the "growth" broker, the one company broker, the institutional broker, the contrarian, etc. Where do they fit in?

Many of these labels refer to variations of the types already discussed; others denote the type of stocks particular brokers fancy; that is, they specify the product sold rather than a distinct market philosophy. Nevertheless, a brief word on each may be helpful.

There are salesmen who deal mainly in options or in OTC stocks who could be called option or OTC brokers. In style, however, they cover the same range of types discussed above, with Action and Customer Salesmen approaches being more dominant.

Institutional brokers, or more correctly institutional salesmen, represent yet another variation. By and large, institutional salesmen are just like their retail counterparts; rather than dealing with individual investors, however, they deal with institutional investors – mutual funds, trust departments, etc.

The situation is somewhat different with the so-called "go-go" broker, the growth broker and the one company broker. These labels generally apply to a specific type of broker. The "go-go" broker of the sixties was basically either a Customer/Action or an Action/Customer broker, going with the most volatile stocks, often as a result of hearing a story. The growth broker is generally a Firm/Customer or a Customer/Firm Salesman who pushed the glamor stocks based upon either firm recommendations or secondary information; often he relies on both types of materials. The one company broker, the broker who tends to push a single stock or a few stocks all the time, is in most cases a sub-type of Customer Salesmen. Generally, he has established contacts within the company and uses these contacts to sell the company; he differs from most Customer Salesmen in that he focuses less attention upon the needs of his customers and more upon his sources of information.

The contrarian, finally, is probably the most talked about non-type of the market. A number of Firm Salesmen and

Customer Salesmen like to claim that they trade *against* the major trends of the market. In most cases, this is more rhetoric than fact.

All market professionals are not in either retail sales, institutional sales, research or management. There are also specialists, floor traders, and money managers. What about them? Again, with few modifications, I think that they can be categorized in terms of our basic types, though you are likely to find a greater number of true believers.

The reason why specialists, floor traders, and money managers tend more to be true believers than either retail or institutional brokers, is that they are judged more in terms of their market performance than in terms of sales. Consequently, they tend to be more interested in actually mastering the market. It should be noted, however, that more recently there has been a decided shift in this emphasis as far as money managers are concerned; more are being judged in terms of the amount of money under management rather than market performance per se.

As a result, more money managers are hedging their bets; that is their investment strategy is being determined more by what others are doing and by the wishes of their clients. A few years ago, a money manager who was very bullish would more likely than not be fully invested even if most of the competition was bearish. Today, he is more likely to be content with being merely more heavily invested than the competition. In short, he is not out to do the best that he can, but to do better than the others. Similarly, whatever his own reading of the market, he is likely to give much more weight to the feelings of his customers. In both cases, this "new" approach is the result of more customers being concerned with the overall relationship with their portfolio managers rather than with market performance as such. This has forced even the most market orientated of money managers to stress their own sales techniques to a degree which was not common a few years ago.[5]

The primary objective of this chapter has been to comment on some of the ways in which the types presented earlier fit together. What we have found is that despite differences in nomenclature, market phases, and relative numbers, the market is constituted by the basic types presented in earlier chapters. We have also seen, however, that market participants can change from one type to another type. The net result of all of this has been to further underscore the ambiguous character of the market.

Unfortunately there remains yet another "type" to be introduced: The Follower.

In light of everything that has been said up till now it may appear perverse to suddenly introduce a new type. If the follower were truly a new type, I think I would have to agree. In fact, however, the follower is not so much new as an amalgamation. Consequently, it is in confronting the Follower that we most directly confront the mind of the market. In order to do this we must turn our attention to the 'crowd syndrome' of the market.

14

The Crowd Syndrome: The Followers

Nearly everyone who has written anything about the market has at one time or other confronted the 'crowd syndrome' of the market. It is an undeniable fact of market life. Even the most sophisticated professional gets caught up in it now and then. In its milder forms it appears as a "fad"; in its more extreme forms as "panic." It can emerge in an up market or a down market. Wherever it appears and whatever its form, its essential character remains the same. Everyone starts to play follow the leader and the leader is screaming 'I must find out where my people are going, so that I can lead them.'

Despite its ubiquitous nature, nearly everyone realizes that getting caught up in such a movement is madness. Nevertheless, every year almost everyone gets caught up in one or more such sequences of events; they become Followers. Why this should be so is another question. A number of different hypotheses have been suggested – emotional contagion, group pressure, repressed anger, etc. – but most prove fairly superficial upon analysis. So, let us take a close look at these instances of mass behavior.

Under normal conditions people act in reference to specific goals and objectives according to specific rules. The goals and rules vary and the actors may themselves be only faintly aware of what they are. The process is admittedly complex and there exists considerable disagreement among "experts" as to the exact nature of the process. Nevertheless, there is general agreement that "meaningful" behavior is rule governed.

This raises the question of where the rules come from. Most theorists answer this question by asserting that the rules are built into our view of the world in which we live. We generally act as if we lived in an "ordered" world.

The specific nature of this order is in turn determined by the perspective or overview that we use. The decision as to what perspective is to be used is in turn generally determined by a wide range of cues which we receive from others. This is what is meant by the common notion that man lives in a social world. We do not give meaning to the world as individuals but rather as a member of specific social groupings.

Though we engage in this process of "defining the situation" continually, it is anything but simple. It entails reading the cues of others, giving off cues ourselves, and a complex process of negotiation. All of this generally occurs without our conscious awareness of what is going on. Nevertheless, the process requires that the participants "believe" that there exists some shared meaning which they can potentially grasp.

There are times, however, when it becomes difficult or even impossible to know what is expected in a particular situation; we are unable to tap into the "shared meanings" which govern what is going on. When this occurs the most common response is to "bluff it." We look about us at others who apparently know what is going on and attempt to mimic their behavior. As the saying goes 'When in Rome, do as the Romans do.'

What happens, however, when no one knows what is going on and everyone is playing follow the leader? The answer is what is generally called "mass behavior." Everyone acts as others are acting rather than in a rational way – in accordance with specific goals and in response to some ordered view of the world. Despite this fact, it is seldom the case that everyone ends up acting exactly the same way. As one person changes his behavior to adjust to what he sees others doing, others are adjusting their behavior in response to what the first person had been doing. As a result, the most common outcome is what could be called the 'milling crowd' syndrome. Everyone adjusting to everyone else without any overall pattern of behavior emerging.[1]

There are times when an overall pattern will emerge and the milling crowd will become a mob.

All instances of joint behavior are, of course, not mobs. There are times when joint behavior *is due* to shared beliefs and/or co-ordinated efforts. These instances, however, are not characterized by the irrationality and impulsiveness associated with mass behavior. This character is due to the fact that mass behavior is not rule governed.

While mass behavior most commonly occurs as a result of a breakdown in social organization – when accepted beliefs are breaking down – it is also likely to occur in situations where there is a lack of accepted beliefs to begin with, or when there is no overall order to any beliefs. It is specifically this latter condition which characterizes the market. The very number of different market theories creates what is basically an ambiguous, unordered situation. The market consequently is always vulnerable to mass behavior; there are times, however, when it is more vulnerable.

Generally, despite the lack of any sort of overall "meaning", most investors act in a meaningful manner. They do this by sticking to their own view of the market, or to the view of professionals who are advising them, and manage to ignore the other conflicting views. As long as their view seems to be working – if they are not making money at least they are not doing any worse than anyone else – they are able to do this. If they get hurt, however, and lose faith in their own view of the market, they are likely to be ripe victims to the dynamics of mass behavior. The less committed they are to begin with, of course, the easier it is for them to lose faith.

The fact that persons in the market are constantly exposed to opposing views is also relevant. Even the most committed of true believers knows that there are other views. He confronts them daily. Consequently, when he gets hurt in the market, he is likely not only to doubt his own market philosophy but also to wonder if the other guys aren't perhaps right.

These factors, I feel, manage to clarify one of the most paradoxical aspects of the market, namely, that the very commitment to make sense out of the market – to discover the mind of the market – often leads to what could be called the 'mindless' character of the market. The instances of mass behavior which are so common in the market would be less likely if the participants attributed more to simple chance and luck. There would always be some who would try to ride with the "hot hand" – those who apparently had luck with them at the moment – but it is doubtful that their numbers would be such as to generate mass behavior. If the general view was that those who were doing very well were simply lucky, it is unlikely that a substantial portion of the not-so-lucky would blindly join in. It is specifically because most participants don't believe that it is simply luck that is at work that draws them in. It is their belief that the market has some sort of meaningful order that leads them to conclude that those who are doing well must "know" something.

There is still the question of "So what?" If your view of the market isn't working, what is wrong with going along with the crowd? If things turn sour for the crowd, at least you will be in good company. There are times when there is nothing wrong with this approach. In fact, if you join the forming crowd early enough, you can do well by simply riding the momentum of the crowd. Unfortunately, the probabilities are that you will not be drawn into the crowd until it has already developed a good head of steam which means that you'll be joining it later rather than earlier. This approach in the long run can spell disaster. First of all, the major move will already have occurred; secondly, you'll find it nearly impossible to extricate yourself from the crowd once you are in it.

There is still the question of why this should be so. If everyone is bullish on the stock, why doesn't it stay up in price? The answer usually given is that while a crowd is right in the beginning, it is wrong in the end. It is right in the beginning because the crowd generates new buyers. Many people may already have bought the stock, but there will be many more who have not. As these others join the crowd, they will push the price of the stock up further. Eventually, however, all who are vulnerable to the pull of the crowd will have bought the stock and there will be no one left. When this happens the only direction left for the stock to go is down. Moreover, it is likely to do this very rapidly since once the balloon has been busted, everyone will want to get out as fast as possible. Those who have joined the crowd later rather than earlier are likely to have to sell for less than they paid.

While there is nothing really wrong with this explanation, it tends to over-simplify and even misrepresent the actual process. It is based on the view that stocks go up when there are more buyers than sellers and down when there are more sellers than buyers. The actual process is more complex than this, especially as it relates to market "panics", whether in buying or selling.

There are never more buyers than sellers or sellers than buyers. For every buyer there must be a seller and vice versa. It takes two to transact. If there is only a buyer or only a seller, there is no trade and, consequently, no price movement one way or the other. It may be argued that the common beliefs regarding the ratio of buyers to sellers refer only to those willing to buy and sell at or near the present price of the stock in question. Ironically, however, if this last position is taken just the opposite relationship holds to that which is commonly assumed. Stocks go up when there are more sellers and down when there are more buyers. In order to understand why this is so it is necessary that we take a closer look at what it means to be a buyer and a seller.

There are always two groups of buyers and two groups of sellers: those willing to buy or willing to sell as the stock moves up and those willing to buy or willing to sell as the stock moves down. (We will ignore those willing to buy and sell at the present price since, in and of themselves, they will not account for any stock movement.) The catch is that only those willing to buy the stock as it moves down can be considered serious buyers *now* since those supposedly willing to buy the stock as it moves up could, if they wanted to, buy it at its present price. Similarly, only those willing to sell the stock as it goes up can be considered real sellers *now,* since those supposedly willing to sell at a lower price could likewise sell now if they wanted to. Those persons who talk about buying a stock as it moves up and those who talk about selling their stock if it moves down are only potential buyers and sellers. Furthermore, in most cases they are only willing to be a buyer or a seller providing the stock moves in such a way that they can buy or sell at a price near the "old price".

Let us assume that a particular stock is trading at 20. The bid/ask is 19⅞ to 20⅛. There is someone who owns the stock who is willing to sell at 20⅛ and there is someone who does not own the stock who is willing to pay 19⅞. One can be considered a potential buyer, the other as a potential seller. The person who is thinking about buying the stock at 20⅛ is only thinking about it as is the person thinking about selling his stock at 19⅞. More specifically, the first person is thinking "If the stock acts well – begins to move up – I think I will buy it if I don't have to pay more than 20⅛." The second person is thinking, "If the stock starts to act badly – it begins to move down – I think I will sell it providing I can get 19⅞." If the first person finds out that he will have to pay 21, he may very well no longer be interested in buying; similarly, if the second person finds out that he can only get 19, he may no longer be interested in selling.

This situation explains one of the paradoxes of the specialist's book – the record the specialist in a stock keeps of potential buy and sell orders. The book contains primarily buy offers below the market and sell orders above the market. Admittedly, it also contains stop-buy orders – orders to buy a stock if it goes up to a certain level – and stop/loss orders – orders to sell if the stock goes down to a certain level; but such orders are fewer in number than the normal buy and sell orders. One might think that many buy orders below the market was a bullish sign since it indicates support for the stock, while many sell orders above the market was a bearish sign since it indicates a heavy supply. In fact, just the opposite is true. Stocks move in the direction of the orders. The fact that there are orders to buy the stock if it goes down makes it possible for the stock to go down as orders to sell the stock as it goes up makes it possible for the stock to go up. If there are no buyers just below the market, few people who own the stock will be willing to sell it: similarly, if there is no stock for sale just above the market, there will be few people willing to buy it.

Admittedly, all of this sounds counter-intuitive, but it makes sense if one tries to understand it in the context of the market. The person willing to sell his stock slightly above the market may be nervous and skeptical about the value of the stock he owns but he still sees the stock as likely to go up in the short term. The person willing to buy a stock as it moves down, on the other hand, may believe in the long term value of the stock but believes that it will go down in the short term. To put this a slightly different way, orders to sell a stock above the market reflect a degree of skepticism in a bullish environment, whereas orders to buy below the market represent confidence in a bearish environment. One only finds significant orders to sell above the market when the market is moving up and significant numbers of buy orders below the market when the market is moving down.

The above analysis also helps to explain why some stocks which move up rapidly stay up whereas others eventually collapse. Furthermore, it sheds some light on the market aphorism regarding "good buying" and "bad buying", "strong hands", and "weak hands".

When the crowd is buying, it is the cooler heads who are selling. As long as there are enough cool heads who are willing to provide stock, the stock is likely to go up. When the crowd owns all the stock, there is no one left to sell. When that happens the stock has peaked. Usually, there are still plenty of people out there willing to buy, but they are not willing to pay any price. It must be remembered that no one in the crowd thinks of himself as a fool. There are limits even when playing follow the leader. It is at this point the aggressive members of the crowd take over.

Throughout an upward movement of a stock, there will always be those who will follow behind; people who will be bidding below the market. As long as there are persons willing to sell their stock slightly above the market to the more aggressive buyers – those willing to pay an extra eighth – the presence of these followers is not felt. When the cool heads are gone, however, there they are waiting to provide the down stairway for the stock. Their optimism is as necessary for the decline of the stock as was the skepticism of the original owners.

The situation with those stocks which maintain their advance is quite different. In their case there is usually some 'rational' reason for the initial move. The crowd view insofar as it exists is normally that the upward move is not justified. Those playing follow the leader begin to sell; it is the cooler heads who are buying. Eventually even those stocks will peak out, but providing a new crowd hasn't formed which now believes the stock will never stop going up, most who now own it will want to own it even if its rapid upward movement should cease for a while. Furthermore, since the crowd view would still be that the stock is, if anything, overpriced, there is not likely to be heavy demand for the stock below the current market.

It is, admittedly, seldom as simple as all this, but the underlying premise that stocks are more likely to go up and stay up if they are moving into "strong" hands, but to go down eventually if they are moving into "weak" hands is generally valid. What it indicates about "strong" and "weak" hands, or "good" and "bad" buying is also true. A strong hand is one which may be willing to sell at a higher price but is unwilling to sell at a lower price; a weak hand is one which is usually afraid to sell at a higher price, but more than eager to sell if the stock begins to decline.

This same analysis also explains why it is a market truism that stocks will nearly always "close the gap". If a stock for some reason "gaps" either upwards or downwards – if it trades at a level significantly different from its last trade – it will usually in the near future retrace its movement to fill in the "gap". A stock, for example, which jumps from 22 directly to 27 is likely to retrace its steps back to near the 22 area before it is able to continue its upward movement. The same would hold true in reverse if it dropped from 22 to 17.

The reason for this is that in the case of the upward movement there will be those who missed it at 23, 24, 25, and 26 who will bid for it below the market, while in the case of the downward movement there will be those willing to sell it if it recovers to 18, 19, 20, or 21. They might have to wait a little while, but sooner or later their impact is usually felt.

It would be wrong and misleading to end this discussion without pointing out that the so-called strong hand is not always the hand of "big" money or the institutional investor; neither do all the "weak" hands belong to individual investors. Despite what Henry Geller – the paranoid apologist presented earlier – says, it is not primarily the amount of money one has to invest. It is the attitude which governs the investment. Anyone playing follow the leader, no matter how much money they have, is a weak hand and represents "bad" buying.

Though the crowd syndrome of the market is primarily due to the ambiguity of the market, there is another factor at work which deserves a mention, namely, the emotional pull of the market. While this might seem to introduce a new element fairly late in the game, it has, in fact, been implicit in the argument from the very beginning. To recapitulate briefly. The crowd syndrome has been explained as due to a general desire on the part of market participants to know what is going on coupled with a plurality of perspectives leading to a pervasive ambiguity which together produce a tendency to play follow the leader since no one knows what is going on but believes that others do.

While this summation is basically correct, it ignores one important question; it does not explain why participants confronted with ambiguity don't just retreat from the whole market. As suggested above this is in fact what most true believers do when they no longer feel confident in their own point of view. It is also fairly clear to anyone who has observed the market over time that many others do the same thing. The question then is why doesn't everyone? The answer quite simply is that they don't want to. They want to be part of the excitement of the market; they get a kick out of the market that they are unwilling to give up. For most it is like being at a large party where they don't know anyone or what is going on, but they don't want to go home.

As might be expected the great majority of these "party goers" are not market professionals; they are rather lay investors. This does not mean, however, that market professionals are immune to the emotional pull of the market. We clearly saw much earlier, for example, that Harry Silver despite being a managing partner of a very prestigious firm still responds to the emotional pull of the market. It is the emotional pull of the market, being part of the public, in fact, which is the thing he most likes about the market. Most market professionals are not as addicted to this aspect of the market as Harry Silver; few, if any, however, are immune to it. Though true believers are least likely to be pulled along, it is a rare true believer who has never succumbed to the magnetism of the crowd.[2]

We began this study with a typical small investor trying to make some sense out of the market. From there we set out in pursuit of the mind of the market. After a fairly lengthy journey we seem to have finally found this mind in what can only be called the 'mindless' quality of the market as a whole. We have managed to shed light here and there, but the total picture still seems to be covered with shadows. We have examined fairly closely a number of different types and their associated views of the market; we have also observed how the various types fit together and merge into each other. We have nevertheless been forced to leave a number of questions unanswered. We have refrained, for example, from actually confronting the question of why this type or that type. It is to this basic question that we now turn.

15

Conclusions: The Uses of Market Knowledge

Three major themes run through this book: (1) the interpretively flexible nature of the market; (2) the dominating and pervasive influence of four basic market philosophies; and (3) the similarities and differences among true believers, salesmen, rationalizers, and followers.[1] To recap:

We began our analyst by underscoring the ambiguity of the market. We noted how the same "facts" can have completely different meanings to different people. It was noted that the problem is not a lack of interpretive schemes, but rather a surfeit of such schemes due to the peculiar responsive character of the market, that is the extreme "self-fulfilling prophesy" potential of the market. More specifically, four basic overviews or philosophies were introduced: The Fundamentalist/Economic view; the Insider/Influence; the Cyclist/Chartist, and the Trader/Market Action view.

The Fundamentalist view was shown to emphasize economic factors: earnings, book value, price/earning ratios, etc. The Insider view was shown to emphasize sponsorship and supply and demand. The Cyclist/Chartist view was shown to emphasize the past patterns of the market and the Trader view was described as focused upon what was called the "life" of the market, or perhaps more accurately, the emotions of the market.

As embodied in the views of their respective true believer spokesmen, these general overviews were shown to entail a number of other things as well. The Fundamentalist/ Economic view defined the market as a given, external, physical reality, governed by "objective," external laws; the market is conceived as controlled – in the long run if not the short run – by economic factors which reflect their own causal logic. This view sees nothing mysterious about the market. Anyone who is willing to work at it can find out what is going on and can thereby master the market. It is a question of work not luck. This pragmatic attitude was revealed not only in statements bearing on what the market was, but also in the types of criticisms that the true believing Fundamentalists made of others, namely, that they were lazy, too emotional, dreamers, etc.

In emphasizing sponsorship and supply and demand, the true believing Insiders define the market in much more interpersonal terms. The market is seen not in terms of products, companies, earnings, etc., but in terms of people, coalitions, decisions, and interpersonal confrontations. This emphasis upon interpersonal relationships is aptly reflected in the major criticism that Insiders are likely to make of anyone, that is, that he or she is dishonest. Furthermore, in attempting to critically assess a piece of information an Insider is more likely to try to see if such action makes sense to him than to look for non-personal supporting data.

To contrast the two approaches with a concrete, if hypothetical situation. If a Fundamentalist was told that the earnings of a company were going to be very low, he would more likely try to get supporting or refuting data bearing on the question than to think through the issue in a hypothetical-deductive manner. An Insider who was told that a major fund was getting ready to take a large position in a given company, in contrast, is likely to try to see if such a purchase makes sense to him given the assets, objectives, etc. of the fund in question.

He may also try to check it out with other contacts, but he is likely, especially if he is a successful Insider, to go very slowly in checking it out in order not to spread the word too soon. It must be remembered that his strength is in knowing how to handle information not just in obtaining it.

In contrast to both Fundamentalists and Insiders, Cyclist/Chartists were shown to be almost mystical in their approach to the market. Keeping charts does not make one a true believing Cyclist/Chartist. One must believe that the market is governed by what could be called a transcendent ordering principle. This concern with a meaningful order is revealed in the way Cyclist/Chartists see other market participants. They see them as basically ignorant; moreover, they see them as generally unable to learn even if they wanted to; they lack the necessary intellectual/spiritual ability.

The real Trader finally was shown not only to see the market primarily in terms of its own life force, but to revel in it. Of all the true believers we met, none approaches the Trader in his "love" of the market. The Trader relates to the market not only cognitively, but emotionally. As far as the Trader is concerned it is impossible to master the market without tuning into one's emotions; on the other hand you can not expect to survive unless you can control your emotions. To give just a brief example of what I mean here, I should like to recount how one Trader responded to my question "How do you decide whether to hold on to a stock or to sell it?" He answered, "I imagine doing both and end up doing what feels better."

Having analysed these various true believers we switched our attention to the salesmen of the market, then to the market rationalizers, and finally to the followers and the crowd syndrome. In each case we were concerned with showing how the four basic overviews were used.

This was most easily done in our analysis of the various salesmen types since each type mirrored one of our true believers. In the case of the market rationalizers and even more so in the case of the followers, these overviews tended to become intertwined; even in these cases, however, it was clear that the market was being defined in terms of one or more of our basic overviews. In short, though the form and mix vary, our analysis of these other market styles showed that the market is continually defined in terms of the basic philosophies of the true believers.

As informative as all of this has hopefully been, it has failed to answer two very basic questions: (1) Why these four overviews? and (2) Why these various styles? We have not dealt with these questions because our objective has been primarily descriptive; that is, I have been primarily concerned with presenting an integrated picture of what the mind of the market looks like. This picture has admittedly, been theoretically structured; moreover, I have repeatedly touched upon these basic "why" questions, especially the first. It is time, however, to deal with them directly, if briefly. I will try to locate each in terms of what may be called our common sense grasp of different forms of "knowing."[2]

The first overview (The Fundamentalist/Economic) is associated with our natural attitude toward the external, physical world, that is the world of objects, causality, rational means/ends order, and external "giveness". The second (Insider/Influence) is related to our world of interpersonal relationships – other wills, relationships of dominance and submissiveness, mutual understanding, and argumentation. The third (Cyclist/Chartist) is related to our symbolic universe of meanings per se where the criteria of conceptual order (consistency, coherency, completeness, harmony) reign supreme, whereas the fourth (Trader/Market Action) is based upon our world of "sensual" experience with its pain and pleasure, emotive tone, and either/or tendencies. Without stretching things too far we could say that the first appears to reach its highest form in modern science, the second in law and legal systems, the third in religion and philosophy, and the fourth in art.

The Market offers us an excellent opportunity to compare these different overviews and the tone of each. In the market we can clearly see the "rational" bias of the economic overview, the "conspiratorial" bias of the political overview, the "compulsive" bias of the ordering overview, and the "intuitive" bias of the market action view.

Initially one might attempt to deal with the second question (why these various styles?) by asserting simply that that is the way things are. As an historical fact this is exactly the way I approached these various styles even after I was well into the study. I might add that I found them an irritating empirical fact of life that was complicating an otherwise fairly straight forward presentation of my four market philosophies. I finally accepted them as part of the market and left it at that. Insofar as the question why true believer, salesman, rationalizer, or follower did crop up, I felt at first that I had answered it in chapters 14 and 15 in terms of relative success. Further thought and re-analysis of my notes and interviews revealed that there was much more to it than this. It showed that true believers, salesmen, rationalizers, and followers as groups looked at the market differently just as those who favor different market philosophies look at the market differently. It was not just a question of how well they had done but rather a question of how they saw the market. This question in turn, was determined by what they accepted as the objective and function of an understanding of the market.

At the risk of muddying water that is rapidly becoming very cloudy, let me state that how and what an individual accepts as the purpose and function of knowledge is not the same as the individual's own purpose. Nearly everyone I ever met in the market was interested in making money in the market. Furthermore, nearly all were interested in getting along with the people they dealt with, with understanding what was going on, and with enjoying themselves as best they could. However, to return to where we began, true believers, salesmen, rationalizers, and followers differ in their views regarding the purpose and function of an understanding of the market.

True believers seek to understand the market in order to master it which means in order to make it work for them. A true believer is intent upon making money in the market;

moreover, he is intent on doing so in terms of a return on his capital. He will take a salary and commissions, but the objective is capital gain. This is true not only of the Fundamentalist but the other true believers as well. The final test of any idea is the extent and degree to which it allows one to master the market. It does not matter how smart he thinks he is; if he knows what he's doing he can prove it by the money he's making.

Salesmen, in contrast, use their knowledge of the market to impress and influence people in order to make sales. They seek to establish some sort of consensus with their customers while at the same time maintaining their position of expertise. They see and use knowledge primarily in a social-psychological manner – as a tool to aid them in interpersonal relationships, rather than as a means for gaining mastery over an "external-non-human" world. As we saw earlier, this is most clearly the case with the Customer Salesmen, but it holds true for the other types of salesmen as well.

The rationalizers main concern, meanwhile, is to make sense out of the market; they want to show that there is some sort of underlying order to the market. Some, like Henry Geller, may take a cynical view of this order whereas others, like Dave Gibbons, may have a more resigned attitude, but in all cases the rationalizers primary objective is to convince you and themselves that there is a basic order to the market. To answer the question posed at the beginning of this paragraph, the key function of market knowledge to the rationalizer is that it provides an "ordered" view of the market.

Formulated in this way, it may sound as if rationalizers are all "closet" Cyclist/Chartists given that a concern with the underlying order or pattern of the market was earlier shown to be their essential characteristic. The difference is that a Cyclist/Chartist deserving to be called a true believer is still primarily concerned with mastering the market. On the other hand, the implication that anyone favoring the Cyclist/Chartist view has a strong propensity to become a rationalizer is correct. We saw this, in fact, with not only Dave Gibbons but also Bob Klein.

This leaves us with thc followers and the crowd syndrome. What function do the various overviews of the market have for them? The answer, I feel, is quite clear. The various explanations and accounts which the followers grasp at as they are pulled along provide them with a sense of belonging, a sense of solidarity with others. The follower does not want to master the market; he does not really want to influence people; he is not searching for "meaning". He wants to be part of the action. In short, the follower is hooked on the same social dynamics of the market that a Trader like John Holland uses to his advantage and Action Salesmen use to their advantage.

In summary, we can see that the same four dimensions used to classify the basic overviews of the market can be used to classify the way these overviews are used.[3] This can be graphically represented as follows:

MATRIX OF STOCK MARKET TYPES

Dimension stressed in use of overview	DIMENSION STRESSED IN OVERVIEW ITSELF			
	Economic	*Political*	*Ordering*	*Libidinal*
Economic	Fundamentalist	Insider	Cyclist-Chartist	Trader
Political	Firm Salesmen	Customer Salesmen	Market Salesmen	Action Salesmen
Ordering	Rationalizer: "all discounted or irrational"	Rationalizer: With conspiritorial tendencies	Rationalizer: Efficient Market Theory	Rationalizer: "Market too complex: too many people"
Libidinal	Greedy Follower	Insecure Follower	Confused Follower	Natural Follower

In addition to giving us a picture of the various market types described in this study, this chart allows us to understand better a number of apparent paradoxes. We saw earlier, for example, that even relatively successful true believing Insiders often end up in sales and that similarly successful true believing Cyclist/Chartists often end up as highly paid rationalizers. We also saw that while it is possible for a true Fundamentalist to go his own way ignoring those about him, a good Trader must keep his hand on the pulse of the crowd. We similarly saw how many successful Firm Salesmen can become almost indistinguishable from true Fundamentalists, whereas even the most competent Action Salesman often appears to be nothing but a player. All of this could be accounted for by a general pull towards what could be called intentional homogeneity; that there is a tendency to define the world in a manner which is consistent with the purposes to which we put this knowledge. The reverse of this is also true, namely that there is a tendency to use knowledge in a manner which is consistent with the basic modality of the knowledge itself.

To talk of the different uses of knowledge in the market is one thing; to attempt to generalize from the market is quite another. It is a truism, for example, that people get involved in the market for all sorts of reasons: the money, the excitement, etc. Consequently, it does not seem to require any great stretch of imagination to accept the idea that people are apt to perceive the market quite differently, and that they are likely to use whatever knowledge they have of the market in different ways. Can one, however, generalize from the market to other spheres of social life? I firmly believe that we can and here I refer not only to the four basic overviews and their respective intentional dimensions, but also to the inherent "rationalities" of these overviews and the various uses of these overviews.

At the race track, for example, some bet on those horses which appear to have the best record of past wins, blood lines, etc. Others like to follow what they consider to be the "smart" money, usually the large bets which come in just before post-time. Others look for clues in the particular number assigned to the horse, the day of the week, or some other series of numbers with which they are familiar. And there are yet others who bet in accordance with their own instinctive response to the animals as they parade in front of the grandstands before the race.

There are some, of course, who prefer to own horses and race them rather than to bet on them. There are others who prefer to take the bets of others and then there are those who write how other people should bet. Finally there are those who just like watching the horses run. Similar example could be presented describing the way people approach and deal with almost anything from a work of art to a crystal dug up from the ground.

There remains, however, one final and very important question. What if anything does the market tell us about the relative priority of these various modalities, "logics", and uses of knowledge? Can we say that one orientation, one logic, or one purpose is more basic than the others? Can we say anything about why one orientation, logic, or purpose is selected over the others? Does the market, for example, shed any light on the controversy among those who argue that the purpose of mind is to reveal the structure of the external world and hence knowledge must be judged in terms of this external reality (the pragmatic outlook), those who argue that mind functions primarily to establish and maintain social order (the ideological view), those who argue that mind is essentially concerned with its own internal order and structure (what might be called the cognitive view), and those who see the prime function of mind as providing very special grounds for human solidarity.[4]

What our analysis of the mind of the market indicates is that it is useless to attempt to select one orientation, one logic or one purpose and ignore the others; it indicates that mind is inherently multi-facet and any attempt to deny this will only lend to an incomplete picture of whatever subject is being studied.

Though this conclusion is basically negative, in tone, it tells us what not to do – it carries with it an implicit positive injunction as well, namely, that we give greater emphasis to mind's social nature. It does so in two ways: (1) to accept mind's multi-facet character, in effect, means to give greater emphasis to its social character since it is specifically this aspect of mind which is most commonly ignored; and (2) to accept this multi-facet character entails placing mind as a whole within a social context because it is only in such a context that the various aspects of mind can be meaningfully integrated. Our analysis of the market would seem to suggest a third reason, namely, that though the mind of the market clearly reflects all four orientations, logics and purposes of mind, the constant pull of the crowd would indicate that mind's social solidarity function may indeed be primary.

The market, of course, remains a fairly unique and distinct place. One must consequently be careful in making too broad generalizations about life in general. Nevertheless, having spent a good number of years observing the market I find it difficult to disagree with John Holland when he says – as he so often says – "The market is one of the best models of life that you are likely to find."

Appendix A: Some Practical Advice to the Individual Investor

I began this book by quoting the market aphorism that 'The only thing clear about the market is that nothing is clear.' I also noted that the reason for this was that different persons defined the market differently. Hopefully the descriptions of the various types and their interrelationships presented above have added some substance to this broad generalization.

To anyone in the market none of this is news. They do not have to be told that the market is confusing nor that they are confused. Most, in fact, are not only confused, they are worried. The descriptions of the various market philosophies and the various types may help to explain the problem, but it certainly doesn't resolve it. There remains the question of what an investor is to do.

There are a number of answers to this question: (1) he can get out; (2) he can get someone else to manage his money; (3) he can attempt to master the market; or (4) he can attempt to 'cut loose.'

Initially, it may seem that to get out would make the most sense. Unfortunately, it seldom works. It doesn't work because the reasons why people become involved in the market in the first place—the desire to make money, to be part of the action, to relieve boredom, etc.—just do not go away. In fact, for most the desires become greater; to make matters worse, most also feel that if they did go back, they would be able to do better than last time. (It should be understood that most who leave, leave having done pretty badly.)

It might be argued that it doesn't matter how one gets out as long as he gets out. But it does matter. The person who is forced out, even when supposedly he made the decision, is always vulnerable to be sucked back in. Here one might counter "Burnt once, twice shy", but as we have seen the market is more subtle than this. "There is more than one way to skin a cat." In the market, each approach represents a potentially new way to "skin the cat". I could cite innumerable examples to support this claim. Here are three.

Ron Henry is in his mid-thirties. He has already quit the market "for good" twice, the first time in the late sixties. For five years he had maintained an active account with an Action broker. During those five years he owned scores of stocks. Some did well; some poorly. After five years, however, he had only slightly more than when he had started and he had been adding money each year. After two particularly bad trades, he had a fight with his broker – he called him a crook among other things – and cashed in his chips. He told me then that he would never go back to the market. "All those guys are croupiers, I'd do better in Vegas."

For close to six years he was good to his word. In 1974, however, he began to take a different position. It wasn't the market that was so bad, but the broker he had had and the approach he had used. In fact, he had concluded that it wasn't even wrong to speculate. The secret was to limit one's losses. Through a friend he had been introduced to a broker in Texas who had worked out an almost foolproof way to make money by selling covered options. By 1975 he was fully invested again. To make a long story short, by the end of 1976, he had quit the market again "for good". I would guess that the next time he will be hooked by a Chartist.

For Sam and Esther – a couple now in their late seventies – the historical background is somewhat different but the end results have been very similar. They first got involved in the market in the twenties. In the crash of '29 they got hurt; not that badly, but enough to convince them that the market was no place to put their hard earned money. In the late forties, however, they decided to give it another try. This time, they promised themselves that they would be more careful. For close to ten years working with a fundamentally orientated broker they maintained a very conservative approach. They made money. Unfortunately, they didn't make nearly as much money as a lot of other people. In the late fifties they had an argument with their broker and switched their account to a broker who was more orientated to trading. Again they made money, but again they ended up having a fight with their broker over a specific trade. They sold all of their stocks and put their money in a savings bank. I had an opportunity to talk to them during this period and they were adamant that they would never invest in the market again. They were convinced that all brokers were crooks. Two years later, however, they were back in the market. This time they were seduced by an apparently very successful broker who had access to a lot of very good "inside" information.

Mary C. first got involved in the market when she bought a stock on the advice of her boss. He had some "good" information on a small West Coast company with which he did business. The situation worked out and she nearly doubled her money – about five thousand dollars – in three months. For the next three years she followed one tip after another. In the process she gave back over half of her original profit. In disgust with herself and her broker – who was her boss's broker – she got out of the market in 1974. By 1976 she was back in again; moreover, she was with the same broker following the same approach. When questioned about this she told me, "Well, even with my losses I still was ahead. I guess that if I want to make money I'll have to learn to take my losses in my stride."

Many people who get out of the market, get back in by way of a mutual fund. Unlike those persons just described, those who invest in mutual funds generally have given up trying to make sense of it. Unfortunately, the results – as far as making money is concerned – are not much different from the results achieved by those who reinvest for themselves. Often they're worse.

One case that comes to mind is that of Mr. and Mrs. Williams. For over twenty years they played the market. During this period they switched brokers a number of times. They never, however, ever quit the market. Even during bad periods, and they had a number, they never "gave up" on the market. They didn't, in fact, really even ever give up on their brokers. Each switch was due more to external circumstances – a move, an introduction to a new broker, etc. – than to their frustration with the broker that they had at the time. In fact, after more than twenty years in the market both felt fairly confident in their own abilities to manage their own money.

With retirement things changed. The contacts and flow of information upon which they had based most of their investment decisions began to dry up. This was followed by one particularly disasterous year in which they lost over twenty per cent of their assets. As a result of these developments, plus their desire to travel more extensively, they decided to sell all of their stocks and to invest in a conservative mutual fund. After eight years with this particular fund, their net assets are less than they were when they began. Others have had similar experiences.

The problem with mutual funds is that professionals are generally no better at mastering the market than the non-professional. Most professionals as we have seen are subject to the same vagaries and conflicts as the individual investor. Moreover, no one manages someone else's money for love. The professional has to make a living, and furthermore, his cut comes off the top. Consequently in order for a mutual fund to do as well as the market as a whole, it must in fact do better.

Despite these drawbacks, it would seem reasonable that at least some funds should be able to do just that. Some do.

Unfortunately, it is pretty much impossible to tell ahead of time which funds will do well and which will not. Just as some stocks will always out-perform the market, some funds will always out-perform it. Some investors attempt to adjust to this situation by trading funds. The "upfront" commissions charged in the purchase of most mutual funds, however, make this a nearly always losing proposition.

Some funds, however, should consistently out-perform the market. Here I have in mind funds managed by a true believer of one sort or another. Historically, most small investors have had access to such true believers only by investing in some fund or other. Unfortunately, even these money managers have been exposed recently to pressures which have diverted them from their original objective. They are being judged more and more in terms of the money they have under management than by their market performance per se.

As a result, as noted above, money managers' investment strategies are being determined more by what others are doing and by the wishes of their clients than by their own evaluation of what the market is likely to do. They are not out to do the best they can, but to do better than the others. This change began primarily with money managers running institutional accounts. It was the institutional investor who first evidenced a desire to beat the competition rather than the small investor whose primary objective remained that of making money. Nevertheless, the small investor has been caught up in this development whether he likes it or not, since even the most market oriented money manager knows that his own job is more dependent upon the amount of money he has under management than upon how well he does with that money. Investment decisions, therefore, are determined with an eye towards future sales of the fund rather than by the actual performance of the portfolio. Onc particularly astute money manager once complained to me that he was actually afraid to outperform the competition "too much".

"A few years ago, if I doubled my money while everyone else did ten per cent, I would have been a hero. Today, if I did the same thing, I'm more likely to be accused of taking unnecessary risks and actually lose accounts."

(Though this view was expressed by more than one money manager whom I interviewed, I must admit that I still find it somewhat difficult to accept at face value. I think that most money managers are more concerned with keeping an eye on the competition than they were, but I can't help feeling that most would still be very happy to outperform the competition significantly even if this meant that they stood out and could be accused of being too speculative. Whatever the real situation most money managers feel a greater need to project an image of soundness as well as an image of brilliance.)

As a consequence of these developments, even if an individual investor is fortunate enough to pick a fund managed by persons capable of mastering the market, the probabilities are that fund managers will be unable to perform up to their full potential. For the individual investor, the bottom line is that his chances of beating the market by having his money in a mutual fund are not any better than they are dealing with a competent retail broker.

So where does this leave us? What is the individual investor to do? The most obvious answer would seem to be that he will have to do it on his own. By and large this is the advice that one is most likely to get from reading any of the numerous books published for the individual investor. For some it is even good advice. Unfortunately, it is also advice which is pretty impossible to follow. Understanding the market is a full time occupation; few have the time. This becomes obvious when you begin to examine what is required. It is necessary to understand not only how the market itself works, but the strategies and style of one's broker and last, but not least, one's own interests and objectives. Here it may seem that I am overstating the case, but let us look at what is actually entailed in such a project.

To begin with, such an individual investor would have to start by familiarizing himself or herself with the "market basics". The best place to start would be the local library or bookstore. While many of the hundreds of books that have been written on the market are not worth reading, there exist a few with which all serious investors should be familiar. My three favorites are Graham and Dodd's *Security Analysis*, Gerald Loeb's *The Battle for Investment Survival*, and Adam Smith's *The Money Game*. In combination, these three books provide a good basis for an understanding of the market; the first and the last also provide bibliographic references to a number of other books for those willing to do additional reading.

The next step would be to spend some time with three or four of the more popular financial publications. If I had to choose three, I would pick *The Wall Street Journal*, *Barrons*, and the financial section of *The New York Times*. Later, if there is time, one could also look at such publications as *Business Week*, *Forbes*, and *Fortune*. It would not be enough to read one or two issues; unlike the books mentioned earlier, these publications do not pretend to give a general view. They focus on current news. If they are to be of assistance in developing an overview of the market, they must be digested over a period of time.

Time. The word was used three times in the last paragraph. The fact is that it requires a significant amount of time to acquire even a superficial understanding of the market. From my own experience, I would say that you would have to plan on an initial investment of at least fifty hours and a continuing investment of between ten and fifteen hours a week. Must one put in this time? Regarding the first fifty or so hours, I would say yes; regarding the ongoing ten to fifteen hours a week, I am less dogmatic. It would be possible after doing your homework for a period of months, or whatever time is required to develop a general idea of what is going on, to cut back on the weekly assignments. This would, of course, make you more dependent upon your broker. If you have a good broker and if your time is limited, this would not necessarily spell disaster. It would mean that you would have to know your broker better than would otherwise be the case.

"Know your broker!" Few rules are more important to the individual investor. Unfortunately, most people know next to nothing about their broker. They may know where he lives, how many children he has, what clubs he belongs to, if he is a democrat or a republican, etc., but few know anything about his market philosophy or his market style. Considering how hard most people work for the money they invest, this is hard to believe, but it is true.

How would one begin to determine the market philosophy and style of his or her broker? To begin with, you would have to have some familiarity with the various major overviews of the market, as well as major types of brokers. Hopefully, this present study could provide the grounds for such knowledge. You would also have to have a general understanding of the market itself which this book and those mentioned above could also provide. All of this, however, would merely be background knowledge; you would still have to come to terms with your own broker.

How could one do this, given that the various types are often difficult to distinguish from one another? It is difficult for market professionals and social scientists to distinguish between similar types; the problems for most lay investors would be greater since they have the added problem of trying to separate their broker's true views from those which he projects as part of his image. Fortunately, the individual investor has an important option open to him; an option which too few ever use. He or she could ask his or her broker to spell out his views. One must, of course, know the questions to ask.

You would have to ask your broker all of the following questions: What types of stocks does he prefer his customers to own? Asset rich companies? Blue chip companies? Growth stocks? Market leaders? Or does he have certain specific companies that he likes to follow? How important does he feel institutional investors are in determining the direction of the market? Is he worried about stock manipulation in any specific situations? Does he believe in market cycles and if so, do these cycles primarily effect the market as a whole or individual companies and industries? Does he give much weight to market timing? What books would he recommend that you read? What periodicals should you keep up with? What does he read? Does he subscribe to any advisory service? How important is the tape to him? Does he follow it regularly? Does he give much importance to any technical indicators such as the "odd-lot" figures or advance and decline ratios? What does he think of most institutional research? What does he think of his own firm's research? What is his attitude toward the use of options? If he thinks they are useful, it is important to determine whether he believes only in selling covered options or whether he is willing to "go naked" or to buy options. What is his attitude toward using margin? Does he prefer his customer to diversify their holding and if so to what degree? What percentage of your assets does he believe should be in the market? What other types of investments would he recommend? What does he think of his fellow professionals? Do most of them know what they are doing? How sophisticated does he believe his own customers are? How does he conceive of your mutual responsibility in making market decisions? Does he enjoy being a broker, and, if not, what would he prefer to be doing? Finally, how does he feel about investing his own money in the market? If he does invest, does he also trade?

Obviously, you could not hope to ask all of these questions in one sitting. You would have to plan on giving this project a considerable amount of time. There would still be the problem of knowing what to make of the answers. You would have to do two things: (1) determine to what degree the broker is a true believer and to what degree a salesman, rationalizer, or just follower; and (2) determine which market orientation he favors. Hopefully, points discussed earlier would be of some help in doing this, but it should be clear that neither job would be very easy.

If one were successful in doing these things, the probabilities are very high that you would discover that your broker was a salesman not a true believer. His primary concern would not be to master the market, but to sell stocks. You could attempt to find another broker who was a true believer, but I am afraid the possibility of being successful would not be very great; there are just not that many true believers and only a minority of them manage retail accounts. This would not necessarily mean failure anymore than finding a true believer would mean automatic success. It does mean that you would have to be very selective in following his advice; you would have to be able to distinguish advice honestly given and a sales pitch. On the positive side, the average salesman, because he is more eclectic, allows the individual investor to follow an investment strategy which may be more in keeping with the investor's own orientation than would most true believers.

To make the best use of your broker, you would have to begin by determing which orientation he is most comfortable with. Since he is unlikely to be a true believer, he will not be wedded to one approach. Nearly all brokers, nevertheless, have their own strengths and weaknesses. Firm Salesmen, almost by definition, are more secure when dealing with stocks recommended by their firm; Customer Salesmen are normally better in evaluating market stories, etc. It should be remembered that all brokers would like their customers to do well; it is clearly good business, and thus for the most part, they try to do their best. It is up to the investor to know what this best is. This can usually be done by analyzing his answers to the various questions presented above. Taken as a whole, his answers should indicate with which approach he feels most comfortable. If and when he begins to push a stock for reasons different from those he normally gives, it is time to be on one's guard.

Does this mean that one could follow one's broker with confidence provided he is consistent? No! It must be remembered that the expertise of any salesman is that he know how to sell. By forcing him to stay with what he knows, one would only insure that the broker would be playing his strong suit; in any suit, however, there are good and bad cards. The broker normally knows which are which. The investor who lets his broker know that he is not only willing but prefers to wait for the right card will more often than not force his or her broker to be more selective than would otherwise be the case.

The effect of following the procedures outlined above would only insure that one would get the best possible service from one's broker. It would still be the broker, however, who would be making most market decisions. This raises the question of whether or not there are other rules which would allow the individual investor a greater say in making market decisions. The answer to this question is yes; for the average investor, however, such rules are of little use. Any rule is only valid as part of a general market approach. Unless an investor is willing and able to put in the time required to develop his own market approach, which few are willing or able to do, it is usually counterproductive to try to second guess one's broker when it comes to the particulars. It is a simple case where a little bit of knowledge can be a dangerous thing.

This doesn't mean that an investor should take a completely passive role in the management of his or her own account, but in order to take a more active role the investor would also have to know himself. This may seem like strange advice since most of us feel that we know ourselves quite well. It must be remembered, however, that I am talking about a very specific type of knowledge. I am talking about knowledge of market philosophy and market style. Few investors have any knowledge of themselves in this regard. They may have some idea of the amount of risk they are willing to take and the amount of return they desire, but what of their general views of the market? Does one see the market in terms of supply and demand or in terms of underlying economic values? Does one feel that the market is inherently ordered or is it governed primarily by chance?

These questions are of fundamental importance to those investors who want to manage their own accounts; the answers should serve as the foundation for developing a market philosophy. They are also important for those who are content to rely upon their broker because the broker-customer relationship is a social relationship, as well as a purely economic relationship. Whatever the ability of the broker or the customer, the relationship will not work unless there is trust and some degree of empathy. I am talking here about market empathy not personal empathy. The most successful true believer will seldom make any money for a customer who is out of tune with him. If he is a Fundamentalist, the customer will become bored and sell just before the long anticipated move; if he is a Trader, the customer may panic at the wrong moment. In contrast, it is often possible to make money with a moderately astute salesman when your market rhythms are in harmony.

To know with what you are comfortable and what you can take is perhaps the most under-rated element within the market. It best explains why so few people are able to follow their own advice. Anyone who attempts to trade, for example, learns very quickly about the need to limit losses, yet there are few who are able to take the "short loss". Similarly, Fundamentalists continually stress the need for patience, yet many are unable to exhibit such patience. The fact is that there are no universal rules; each style has its own rules. The secret is to find a broker whose basic style is compatible with your own style.

In light of the three part program just outlined, it should be clear why few persons could even consider it as an option: most people simply do not have the time. Even if they had the time, I would guess that most would find the whole process disagreeable. It would be one thing if success were guaranteed, but knowing what we do of the track record of even the few true believers of the market, we know this is not so. The possibility of making money in the market following option three is definitely better than following options one or two, but it remains a possibility not a certainty.

Consequently, most individual investors are left with the fourth option – to cut loose.

Initially, it might appear that it should be relatively easy to "cut loose". All that is really required is to avoid the crowd. This, in turn, simply requires ignoring all the nonsense that one hears which should not be too difficult since most people recognize it as nonsense to begin with. In the concrete reality of the market, however, cutting loose is much more difficult than it would appear.

First of all, the crowd is not that easily recognized. There are times, admittedly, when you can almost hear the panic in your broker's voice, when you can see the jump in volume, when you are hearing the same thing from everyone, etc. In most cases, however, the crowd is much more subtle. There is little evidence of panic; the changes in trading activity are not that dramatic; and not everyone is in agreement. Your broker is not telling you that "you have" to do anything; he just feels strongly that you should do it. There may be a general mood to the market, but it is not a ruling passion. It may be seductive, but it is definitely not coercive.

You could avoid even these subtler crowds by ignoring everything that you hear. Such an approach would entail its own costs. By cutting loose, I don't mean picking stocks by throwing darts in your basement. Any "rational" approach to the market requires information of some sort. Even the most astute investor can also generally benefit from some sort of advice. In short, it is generally impossible to be "in the market" without being "in it".

So what can you do? It is necessary to begin by doing some of the same things that those who want to be students of the market do. First, you must generate some personal, coherent view of the market. It can be a relatively simple view and it need not conform to the view of any specific type of true believer. It must have a certain degree of logical consistency, however, and be capable of generating certain rules of market behavior. It does not matter what the rules are, as long as there are some rules.

The need for some set of rules is basic; without them you are lost. Some rules, of course, are better than others. The key, however, is to have rules which can be applied in practice. You should have some rules, for example, regarding the types of stocks you want to own. Such rules can refer to the P/E of the stock, the industry involved, a particular product which you like, its yield, its price range, etc. The specifics are not that important. What is, is that you are able to ask yourself if the stock in question is the type of stock you would like to own. In this regard, it is also useful to have a few rules regarding types of stocks that you do not want to own.

Next, it is useful to have some rules on when you are willing to buy a stock and sell a stock. Again, it does not matter that much what the rules are as long as you apply them in some meaningful way. You might decide that you only like to buy stocks when you have surplus cash, or when a stock has made a new high, or when a stock has gone down twenty-five per cent or more. Similarly, you might decide that you like to sell a stock when it has gone up, or down, twenty per cent, or after you've owned it for six months. The key point again is not how good the rule is but that it is a rule.

To say that it doesn't matter what the rule is may sound silly. Obviously, some rules must be better than others. It must be remembered, however, that the purpose of these rules is not to make you a sophisticated investor. If you want to try that route, you will have to go back to the advice given earlier to those willing to become students of the market and to put in the time required. The purpose of these rules is to protect you from being seduced by the crowd. The function of the rules is not to guarantee a success, but to avoid disaster.

Once you have managed to put together a set of basic rules, the next step is to take a good close look at yourself. This same advice was given to those planning to become students of the market. If anything, it is even more crucial for the less committed investor. Part of this self-examination should deal with your own attitude towards the market – how do you see the market, what does it mean to you, etc. You will already have started this process in formulating your rules, but it is useful to push these types of questions further than the rule information process itself requires. More importantly, you should attempt to judge your own emotional relationship to the market. For the "casual" investor this is more important than the self-knowledge which bears on market philosophy per se.

What does it mean, however, "to judge your emotional relationship to the market?" Are you a nervous investor? Are you always afraid that your stocks are going to go down? Or, do you tend to be too complacent? Do you sit back quietly as your stocks go down telling yourself that they are bound to recover sooner or later? How greedy are you? Are you happy with a ten per cent return or do you expect to double your money? Do you like it when your stocks are on the most active list, or does it make you uncomfortable? The purpose of all of these questions is to enable you to have some idea as to when you are likely to be most vulnerable to the pull of the crowd, which in most cases will be when you are uncomfortable.

Once you have done these things, you should be ready to confront the market itself. Here, you must remember, (1) that the market is characterized by a number of different philosophies, (2) that most brokers are salesmen not market experts, (3) that the market as a whole is always susceptible to mass psychology, and (4) that while you want to make money, the major thing is to avoid getting wiped out.

With all of these points in mind, the first thing to do is to set limits on the types of information you are willing to receive. You will obviously need and want some types of information and even advice, but most of what is offered you will not want. The specific types of information and advice that you will want will depend upon the rules you have set for yourself and what you know about your own strengths and weaknesses.

If you have decided to limit your investments to low P/E stocks, you do not want to hear about any high flyers no matter what your broker or your brother-in-law has heard. Similarly, if you have decided to sell any stock that declines by twenty per cent, you don't want to know that a big mutual fund has started to buy the stock. If your broker continues to give you such information and advice, after you have told him not to, get a new broker.

On the other hand, you should expect to be told those things which you want to hear. If you are very conscious of yield, you want your broker to tell you if there has been an announcement of a dividend increase. Similarly, if you have told your broker that you don't like buying stocks which sell for less than $10 a share, you want him to remind you of that fact when you tell him that you are thinking about buying a $5 stock.

It is very possible, if not probable, that by doing this you will ignore some good advice and be talked out of some sound investments, but you will also be protecting yourself from getting involved in situations which you are not capable of handling. Keeping a check on your own emotional state is more difficult. Self-analysis doesn't work very well under the best of circumstances; in the market, with its high emotional tone and the need to make rapid decisions, it is often useless. It is hard to tell, when the adrenalin is pumping, if you are nervous because you are afraid that the stock which you own, which has gone up fifteen per cent in two days, is going to give it all back tomorrow, or whether you are greedily waiting for it to double within the week. Nevertheless, there are some precautions that you can take.

One of the best is to play "if, then" games with yourself. In the example just given, try to sit back for a moment and ask yourself, "How will I feel if I don't sell it and the stock collapses tomorrow and gives back its move?" Likewise, "How will I feel if I do sell it and it doubles within the week?" In both cases, you'll probably not feel very good, but it is likely that you will feel like kicking yourself more in one situation than the other, because in that case you'll feel like you should have "known better". You will have gone against your own rules no matter how ambiguous they might be.

Such "if, then" games can and probably should be played before taking any action at any time. It is amazing how often one discovers things one didn't expect. You are thinking about buying a company, but aren't particularly enthusiastic. The thought of it going up and you not owning it, however, makes you very angry. Here, your emotional response has served to make you apparently "unemotional", but the "if, then" game would reveal what is really going on. In another situation, you find yourself biting at the bit to buy a certain stock, but when you compare how you would feel if you missed the move with how you would feel if the situation didn't work out, you find that you'd be more upset if the situation didn't work out.

It would be nice if it always worked out so nicely, but it doesn't. There are times when it is impossible to get a reading on oneself even after playing such mental games. There are times when both options make you feel like kicking yourself as there are times when you could live with either option. In the later case, it generally doesn't matter what you do; in the former, you are better off getting out, or avoiding getting in. You are simply off-balance and vulnerable for a fall.

The need to avoid acting when you are off-balance has other applications. You are likely to be most off-balance and hence most vulnerable after taking a reverse or having made what you consider to be a mistake. This can happen in a number of different ways. The failure to buy a stock which proceeds to double; sitting with a stock which collapses; failure to take profits on a speculative run up, etc. The examples are many: moreover, most people know, after the event, when they have made a mistake and when they are hurting. What they often don't recognize is the extent to which their next decision is influenced by such reversals.

I can remember one personal experience many years ago where I had sold a stock too early. It had had a good move and I was nervous, so I sold it though it had shown no evidence that it was about to collapse. Three days later it continued its upward movement – without me – and I sat there kicking myself. Without really realizing what I was doing, I then proceeded to take the money and invested it in another situation which I had not really been following. It wasn't a bad investment, but it was not, in light of the approach I was using, of the same quality as the one I had sold out of. In fact, I made some money from it. Nevertheless, what I did was a mistake and it cost me much more money than I made. As things turned out, three days later the original stock had a two day correction during which time it came back to about the area where I had sold it. In terms of the overall action of the market it continued to be a stand out; in short, it was a buy. Unfortunately, I didn't have any money left since I had in a rebound action put it all in another stock. I could not sell the stock I had just bought because it wasn't acting badly either. So there I was locked out of the one stock I should have owned.

It could be argued that I should have sold the stock and bought back into the first stock. In hindsight maybe, but even forgetting the extra commissions I would have had to pay, the fact of the matter is that I was off-balance and I knew it. If I did anything it was likely to be a mistake. Rather than giving myself a little time to regain my balance, I had acted hastily with the result that I was more off-balance then than I had been three days earlier.

From what has been said, it should be clear that the act of cutting loose does not mean becoming a contrarian. There is obviously some similarity in the two postures but they are not the same. Each is intended as a means of avoiding the crowd, but in most cases the so-called contrarians constitute a crowd themselves, or at least, their actions are controlled by the crowd almost as much as if they were part of it, though admittedly in reverse.

The logical flaw in the contrarian's position is that it focuses attention upon the action of the crowd rather than the crowd itself. As noted earlier, the crowd may be right; in fact, in the beginning it usually is. To try always to go against the crowd is the same as always trying to go against the tide and that makes little sense. There is nothing wrong with going in the same direction of the crowd provided that you are not part of it and you can control your future actions when the crowd goes off in another direction.

In point of fact, most so-called contrarians are not that

contrary to begin with. Given the nature of the market – with everyone normally going in different directions – it is pretty difficult to determine what is the dominant mood. On the same day that I have been informed by one self-annointed contrarian that he is buying, I have been informed by another that he is selling. The only way to avoid getting caught up in a crowd is to maintain one's own council; to be true to oneself and one's own rules of market behavior.

I have already touched on some of the reasons why this is so difficult. There are all of these conflicting views which generate an ambiguity which nurtures mass behavior. There are also all of those salesmen pushing you this way and that, to say nothing of one's own greed and fear. There is another factor at work. Despite claims to the contrary, the market tends to generate an image of itself which makes joining the crowd not look that bad. At times it even makes it look comforting if not actually wise. It may be simply a case of giving people what they want, but it has its own effect nevertheless.

This might seem to be a "cheap" shot, but look at the image that the market, or rather those persons running the market, project. Merrill Lynch is "Bullish on America!" and what image do they give us? American industry at work? No! A herd of steers running along together. They don't even give us a good bull. And then there is E. F. Hutton's "What does your broker say?" "Well, my broker is E. F. Hutton (which, of course, is not true since his broker is really either Al, Fred, or Mary) and E. F. Hutton says . . . ", followed by everyone trying to hear what E. F. Hutton has to say.

Even something as innocuous as the 'most active list' feeds into this syndrome. For some (primarily traders) the most active list is of central importance. For most, it has little if any real importance. Nevertheless, they are always on prominent display. In fact, the market is always playing up the crowd and suggesting that if you get with the "right" people and/or the "right" stocks you'll be okay. I am not saying that this is their intent, but it is definitely part of the effect.

So far in this Appendix I have been stressing the seductive

nature of the crowd and some general precautions that one can take to immunize oneself. At the risk of oversimplifying things, I think it is time to get a little more specific, though it is difficult to lay down specific market rules which will work for all people at all times. Different strategies require different rules. Nevertheless, there are I believe, four which nearly everyone should attempt to follow. There is nothing "holy" about them in and of themselves; the purpose of these rules is to aid one in following the more general advice presented above, namely, to be true to yourself, to think for yourself, and, most importantly, to avoid being seduced by the "crowd".

(1) Invest in situations which you can understand. What I mean by this is that you have some clear idea as to why you think the stock should go up in price. It may be that you believe that new management will be able to turn a company around, that you see an increased demand for a particular product, that you see an interest in a particular industry, etc. Your specific reasons are not important; what is important is that the reasons are your own. Only if you have an understanding of why you intend to do what you intend to do, can you judge when the situation has changed and another decision is required. In short, you must know what factors are relevant to your decision and which factors are irrelevant.

(2) Take the short loss. This rule is followed by all True Believers, though they formulate it in different ways. You cannot hope to be successful in the market if you allow yourself to sustain substantial losses. A fifty per cent decline in assets requires a double, just to get even. Tomorrow will always offer new opportunities, but you will be unable to take advantage of them if you have nothing to invest. Furthermore, you may never regain your balance. A large loss is bad enough in itself, but more often than not it makes you vulnerable for even greater losses.

How, however, is one to do this? The simplest way would be to set a limit in your own mind – let's say a ten per cent loss – and to stick to it. If the stock declines by ten per cent below your purchase price, you sell. The simplest way, however, is not always the best way. The ten per cent limit notion is in most cases too rigid. It is better to set a specific price – usually within or close to the ten percent limit – below which you feel the stock should not fall if your initial evaluation of the situation is correct. Ideally, you should have a reason for picking the price you pick. The most common, and probably the best, reason for setting a specific price is that the stock has in the past been supported at that level; it has not gone below that price in the recent past.

Often it is the case that you cannot find such a support level within the ten per cent limit. If that is the case, you should seriously reconsider your original decision. The fact that a stock goes down a few points is generally not sufficient reason to sell it. You want some indication that the stock is not behaving properly. The violation of support levels is such an indication. On the other hand, it is generally unwise to put yourself in a situation where you will have to sustain a major loss before such a support level is penetrated.

Once you have determined the price below which you will not carry a stock, you must stick to it. There will be times when a stock will penetrate a support level only to turn around and come charging back. The one time it does not, however, is enough to ruin you.

There are times when you may be fortunate enough to have two support levels within the ten per cent limit. You buy a stock at 54 with a near term support level of 52 – it bounced off 52 twice during the last two weeks – and a longer term support level at 49 – 49 has been the low during the last nine months. In such a situation you could play it very cautiously and sell if the stock broke the 52 level or you could hold it. If you elect to hold it, however, it is silly to then sell the stock at 50½. Once it breaks the 52 level, your new support level is 49.

If you watch the market closely and have a good broker with whom you stay in daily contact, you may be able to follow this rule by simply keeping your "sell price" in mind. For those less involved in the market, it is generally advisable to take more concrete steps. Historically, the "stop-loss" order has been the most common way to do this. You would enter a specific order with your broker to sell the stock if it hit a specific price. This is still a good technique in many situations. The emergence of the option market, specifically "put" options, provides another way of handling this situation.

A "put" option can be looked on as a form of insurance. To use the example noted above. After buying the stock at 54, you could buy a 50 put option. The option, which gave you the right to sell the stock for $50 during the time period of the option, would cost perhaps a 1¼ to 2½ depending on volatility and expiration time. In this way you could insure that you could always get $50 back on your original $54 investment.

There are both advantages and disadvantages to using the option approach over the short-loss approach. One disadvantage is that it will normally cost you a little more. A second disadvantage is the price at which the option may be exercised will probably not be exactly the same price that you would have selected based upon past support levels. Thirdly, if you sell a put option as a hedge against a stock, you cannot normally treat the underlying stock as a long term hold. Finally, the stock you are interested in may not have a put option. On the positive side, the option route gives you much more flexibility than a stop-loss order. With a stop-loss order, once your stock has penetrated its support level you are out. With a put option, you can wait and see what happens. If the stock keeps going down – let's say to 45 – and your option is about to expire, you can still exercise your option and get $50 for your stock. On the other hand, if the stock goes down to 47 and then comes back to 54 or even 58, you can let it expire and you will still own the stock.

The option route allows for another alternative. Let us assume that the stock declines to 45, but that it did so as the result of a very bad market or some other factor which really has nothing to do with the stock. Furthermore, let us assume that during this decline it twice ran into major buying at the 44 level which happens to be the low of the stock during the last three years. In such a situation, you may decide that you would like to own the stock. If that was the case, you could sell your put option for approximately $5 which, in effect, would lower your original cost to $49. Admittedly, you would be stretching the ten per cent rule a little, but not so much as to make such a decision untenable.

There are other ways one can use options as a form of insurance. Anyone attempting to use options in this way, however, must make sure that they understand what they are doing, and remember what their basic objective is, namely, to protect themselves from a ruinous loss.

(3) Don't be afraid to make money: Ride your winners. Rule three is really a corollary of rule two. Just as you should not be complacent with a loser, you should not be scared of a winner. As long as you think a stock is worth as much or more than its selling price, you should hold it. But how much is it worth? That is for you to determine and brings us back to Rule 1.

Unless you are only interested in income, it doesn't make much sense to buy a stock at 25 if you think it is only worth 25. You buy stocks which you think are worth more than their current selling price. How much more? Again, it depends upon your overall strategy, but for most people, given the inherent risks in any investment and the unavoidability of some losses, it makes little sense to invest in a stock unless you can see a fifty per cent move somewhere in the near future (six months to a year).

The problem for most people, and it is a problem, arises when they get twenty of that fifty per cent. The tendency to grab your profits and run is very great. When this happens, you must ask yourself "Is the stock worth what it is selling for?" If the answer is yes, don't sell.

If the stock reaches the goals you had set, the situation, of course, is quite different. Unless the situation has changed in such a manner to make you increase your expectations (I am talking about real reasons which make sense to you not simply the fact that the stock has reached your original goal) the stock can be sold. Similarly, if you are forced to conclude that your original judgment was over-optimistic, you may want to sell at a lower price than you initially contemplated. The key in all situations is to sell only when you believe the stock deserves to be sold.

Your reasons for deciding when a stock is fully valued will depend upon the particular market philosophy that you adopt. Regardless of your reasons or what price you select, you should have a clear objective in your mind when you buy a stock just as you should have a clear idea of what type of loss you are willing to sustain. Here an option strategy can be useful.

From what has been said, it should be clear that I don't recommend buying a stock at 27 and selling a call option at 30. Certain traders can play this game using short term options, but it requires more time and sophistication than most investors have. On the other hand, if the stock advances to the mid-thirties, it may make very good sense to sell a 40 call option. Such an option may serve as insurance against greed just as a put option can function as insurance against fear and/or complacency. The extra money that you will receive for the option is always welcome, though it obviously won't be much, but, more importantly, it will force you to seriously reconsider your position if the stock reaches 40. Rather than ignoring what is happening, you will be forced to decide whether you are willing to let someone else take your stock at 40, or whether you would rather, in effect, repurchase the stock at these levels by buying back your option. Whatever you decide, you must remember that the main function of the option is not to earn you a few extra dollars but to insure that you maintain some sort of rational orientation towards your stocks.

(4) "Use market orders. There are some very sophisticated investors who rely very heavily on limit orders. Furthermore, there are situations which almost seem to demand limit orders. Nevertheless, as a general rule for most investors, "Use Market Orders" is sound advice.

Initially, it might appear as if Rule 4 contradicts Rules 2 and 3. Isn't a stop-loss order a limit order? Did I not say that you should set specific prices for yourself? Isn't that just what a limit order does? The answer to the first question is "No." A stop-loss order is not a limit order. Once the stop has been hit, your stop-loss order becomes a market order. (There is such a thing as a stop-loss limit order, but this is not the type of order that is being recommended.)[1] Similarly, setting a specific price in one's mind is not the same thing as using a limit order. Once your stock reaches the price you have set, you should act even if you do not get the exact price you want. With limit orders this might not happen; rather than forcing you at act, limit orders often cloud the issue and allow you to procrastinate.

Rules 1, 2, and 3 all have one basic objective: to force you to have a clear and defined idea of what you expect the stock to do, as well as a clear commitment to do specific things in response to the way the stock performs. They should also protect you from being thrown off balance. In short, in combination, Rules 1, 2, and 3 should tell you whether a stock should be bought, held, or sold. Though limit orders can theoretically be used to support decisions arrived at in this manner, in fact they have just the opposite effect. People use limit orders more as a hedge than anything else. The stock is up to 42 and you are not sure if you really want to sell it or not, so you put in a limit order to sell at 43; or, the stock is down to 17 and you are nervous but you know that it might come back, so you put in a stop-loss order to sell at 16.

If a stock should be sold, it should be sold. A quarter of a point here or there will not change the situation. Similarly, if a stock deserves to be bought, it deserves to be bought. Orders should follow decisions; the order should not be allowed to make the decision for you. Admittedly, you can decide to sell at a specific price and enter a limit order, but as a general practice the use of limit orders has the debilitating effect of allowing you to avoid making decisions.

Are these all the rules one needs? Obviously not. They are the only rules that I know of, however, which I think can be recommended to everyone. Those interested in more specific rules which apply to specific market philosophies can find them earlier in this book. However, I have stressed these rules, because I have reached the conclusion that the mind, or rather minds, of the market is not what is of prime relevance to the average investor. He should have a familiarity with it, but he need not master it. His problem is rather the mindless character of the market which the very plurality of views tends to generate.

I could go on for pages detailing how unrelenting is the pull of this mindless character of the market, even on supposedly sophisticated investors who should know better, but, unfortunately, I have not got the time – I just heard that a major oil company is thinking about taking over a small eastern coal company, which has been acting well lately, and I want to check the story out with one of my neighbors whose brother-in-law has a franchise with the oil company, before I call my broker to find out what he thinks.

Appendix B: A Selected Glossary of Stock Market Terminology

Account: Refers to either a specific customer or "account" of such a customer. Many customers maintain a number of distinct accounts: cash accounts, margin accounts, short accounts, etc. See also *Discretionary Account* and *Street Account*.

Account Executive: Label used for a stock broker by some firms and individuals; may be applied to both retail and institutional brokers.

Accumulation: Describes the process where supposedly large, sophisticated investors, usually institutional ones, are buying a particular stock over a period of time. Normally considered to be a 'bullish' sign for the stock. See also *Distribution*.

Action: Refers to the up and down characteristic of the market; also the excitement and drama of the market. Used often in such expressions as 'tape action' and 'market action.'

Advice: Euphemism used to denote process where brokers make market decisions for their customers.

Advance/declines: Technical term used to compare the number of stocks which have advanced in price as compared to those which have declined in price. A widely used technical indicator.

American Stock Exchange: The second of the two major stock exchanges that is located in New York. Generally is the exchange in which smaller companies are traded. See also *New York Stock Exchange*.

Analyst: A person who is employed primarily to research and evaluate companies. Some analysts also maintain a few of their own accounts, but most work strictly on a salary basis and do not have any direct sales responsibilities.

Ask; Asking Price: See *Bid/Ask*.

Back Office: Refers to that segment of a firm which has little or no direct relationship with the public but is responsible for nearly all "housekeeping" chores.

Bears: Name applied to those people who tend to have a negative view the market, i.e., they think the market is likely to go down. All individuals can be "bearish" at times, but there are some who are perennially so.

Bear Trap: Expression used to describe temporary market decline which stimulates selling or shorting followed by a significant advance in the market.

Bell: (Opening Bell/Closing Bell) Refers to the bell which is sounded to open and close trading on the New York Stock Exchange.

Beta: Technical term for the volatility of a stock. Stocks which fluctuate a great deal will have a high beta and will be considered high risk stocks.

Bid/Ask: Expression used to denote the current price someone is willing to pay for a particular stock – the bid, and the price someone is willing to sell the stock for – the ask. Under normal conditions the bid/ask will fractionally bracket the last transaction, i.e., if the last sale was at 25, the bid/ask is likely to be 24⅞ to 25⅛. In an advancing market, however, it may jump to 25¼ to 25½. Similarly, in a declining market it may drop to 24⅞ to 24½. See *Quote*.

Big Board: Term used to refer to the New York Stock Exchange.

Blocks: Used to refer to large transactions, i.e., transactions usually involving more than ten thousand shares of stocks at a time.

Block Houses: Label given to firms which specialize in trading large blocks, usually for institutional investors.

Blue Chips: Label given to those companies which are well capitalized, have a proven record of earnings, and pay a reasonable dividend.

Bond: A financial instrument which entitles someone to a fixed rate of return for a specific amount of money lent for a specific period of time. A bond does not carry with it any sense of ownership.

Book Value: Phrase generally used to refer to the net value per share of common stock which is determined by subtracting all debts and priority claims from the net assets carried on the balance sheet of the company and dividing by the number of common shares.

Bottom: Term used to denote the lows set by the market. Technicians often like to talk

about double and triple bottoms, which signify that the market has held at a certain point twice or three times. See *Support Level.*

Boxing: Selling against the box. A process whereby someone sells short a stock which they own, using the stock that they own as collateral. For tax reasons, however, the brokerage firm executing such an order must either use its own stock or borrow stock to sell, creating thereby two separate transactions. A widely used technique to avoid incurring a tax liability within a given fiscal year.

Breakout: A term used usually by technicians to indicate that a stock has moved into a new, higher trading range.

Broker: Label given to those employed by market firms whose primary duty is to sell stocks and otherwise service accounts.

Bull: Opposite of *Bear*. Person who believes that market is going up. A bullish attitude is one which reflects such a view of the market.

Buy Order: What it says: an order to buy a stock. See *Market Order and Limit Order*.

C.D.: Certificate of Deposit. Basically an unsecured note of a bank, issued for a limited period of time at a rate slightly under the prime rate, usually in denominations of $100,000.00.

Call: The right to buy a stock at a predetermined price. See *Options* and *Puts*. Such rights are sold as if they were stocks.

Capital: Term used to refer to moneys used for investment purposes as well as moneys already invested in a corporated structure.

Capital Gain/Loss: Profit or Loss resulting from sale of some security or other capital asset. See *Long Term Profit/Loss* and *Short Term Profit/Loss*.

Cash Account: An account in which all transactions must be settled in full on a cash basis within a specific period of days, normally five working days.

Cash Equivalencies: Used to refer to financial instruments such as Treasury Bills and corporate paper, usually with brief duration, which are treated as if they were cash.

CBOE: Chicago Board Option Exchange. The first and still major, option exchange.

Chartist: Name given to person who follows charts. Only a few so-called Chartists are, in fact, True Believers in the Cyclist-Chartist credo. Most so-called Chartists simply use charts as their main selling tool.

Charts: There are numerous different types of charts. In all cases, however, they graphically record various aspects of past market activity, such as price, volume, in an effort to discover market patterns.

Churn: Name given to process whereby a broker constantly buys and sells stocks for an account generating commissions for himself.

Closed-End Fund: Name given to a type of investment fund which issues a specific number of shares and which can be bought into only by purchasing such shares. See *Open-End Fund*.

Commercial Paper: Similar to Certificate of Deposit, except that it is issued by corporations.

Commissions: The fee charged by a brokerage firm for

buying or selling stocks. For most investors, this fee ranges between 1 and 1½ per cent of the sums involved. Of this sum, the broker keeps between 25 per cent and 40 per cent with the rest going to the firm. See also *Negotiated Commissions*.

Contrarian: A person who tends to act in opposition to the dominant mood of the market. Many market professionals like to think of themselves as contrarians but few, in fact, are.

Convertibles: Refers to a range of securities, usually bonds, which are convertible to common stock at a set price normally 10-15 percent above the market price of the stock when the bond is issued. Normally convertibles are offered at an interest rate below the going rate since the owner has an opportunity for capital gains if the stock of the company appreciates in value sufficiently to make the convertible options worthwhile.

Correction: Term used to explain decline in market which is seen to be in an upward move. It is a Wall Street aphorism that the market never goes straight up or straight down. See *Technical Rally*.

Cover: To cover. Term used to name process whereby a person buys a stock or an option which he has previously sold without owning it. See *Shorting*.

Crash: Sudden and large market decline.

Curb: The Curb. Name for the American Stock Exchange which originally did business on the street in front of the New York Stock Exchange.

Cycles: Term used most often by Cyclist-Chartists to indicate the rhythmic character of the market.

Cyclicals: Term used to refer to the stocks of such basic industries as steel, chemicals, etc. which generally move in tandem with economic cycles.

Discount House: Firm which charges lower commissions for executing market transactions than the pre-May, 1975 minimum set rates of the New York Stock Exchange. See *Negotiated Rates.*

Discretionary Account: An account where the broker has been given a limited power of attorney to manage the account.

Distribution: Term used to signify that a large sophisticated investor is selling stock to less sophisticated small investors. Normally considered a bearish sign for a stock. See *Accumulation.*

Diversification: Practice of investing monies in a number of different stocks as a form of protection in case one stock does very badly.

Dividend: The amount of money which is paid pro rata to the owners of shares of a company. This money, which generally comes from the earnings of the company, is likely to vary with the fortunes of the company.

Dow; The Dow: A major stock market index based upon thirty leading blue chip stocks. More accurately, it is the 'Dow Industrial Index'. There is also a Transportation Index and a Utility Index, based respectively upon a number of leading transportation stocks and utility stocks.

Down and Out: An expression used to describe a specific type of "limited risk" call option, traded by only a limited number of Wall Street firms. It generally entails a variable premium for a period of six months with the striking price approximately the currect

	market price. If, however, the stock declines 10 per cent the option becomes void regardless of the subsequent action of the underlying stock. There is also a refund clause if the option is exercised within the first five months. See *Options* and *Up and Away*.
Down Tick:	A transaction which occurs at a lower price than the previous transaction of the stock in question.
Earnings:	The amount of money earned by a particular company. Such earnings are generally stated as per share earnings, i.e., the amount of money earned by the company for each share.
Economy:	General term used to cover the combined activities of all institutions involved in the economic life of the country.
Efficient Market Theory:	Theory that states that the market responds so quickly to all information that the price of stocks at any time reflects their true value at that time.
Exchange:	Terms generally used to refer to either of the two major stock exchanges: The New York Exchange or the American Exchange. Could also be used to refer to any of the various regional exchanges. Chicago, Pacific, Philadelphia, Boston, or Midwest Exchanges. All but the Boston Exchange are engaged in option trading.
Exercise price:	The same as *Striking price*. The price established for buying or selling the underlying stock for a particular option.
Fed:	Term used to refer to the Federal Reserve Bank which controls interest rates and the amount of money in circulation.
Firm:	Colloquial label used to refer to a broker-

The Firm: age institution; used interchangeably with "House." As an adjective, the term "firm" means that a bid won't disappear, in the immediate future.

Floor Broker: A member of the exchange who actually trades on the floor of the exchange. It can refer to persons trading for their firms and/or the public customers of the firm; to persons trading for themselves (though there are fewer of this type now than in the past), or to persons executing trades for other firms (this group is often called "two dollar brokers.") See also *Specialist*.

Fundamentals: General term used to refer to basic economic factors pertaining to a company or the economy in general such as earnings, dividends, capitalization, debt.

Funds: Name given to any of a range of institutions which invest other people's money. Individuals or institutions give their money to such funds and allow the funds to invest their money as they see fit.

Gap: Term used to describe situation where a stock opens at a price significantly different from its closing price.

Glamor Stocks: Name given to any of a number of stocks which generally have a record of growing earnings, a high degree of sophisticated technology, high volatility, and which generally trade at a high multiple of earnings.

Go-Go Fund: A fund which has a history of buying mainly glamor stocks and other high risk-high reward, volatile, stocks. Such funds were very popular in the sixties; they are not so popular today.

Good Buying: Buying which originated with persons or

institutions that have a reputation for being right more often than wrong. Often it is not so much that they are right as it is that they have a lot of money to invest.

Growth: The term used to indicate that a company is expanding and can consequently be expected to have higher earnings in the future.

Gun Slinger: Term used to refer to persons who go after highly speculative situations. Again, much more popular in the sixties than today.

Head and Shoulders: Chartist's expression used to describe a specific trading pattern which graphically gives the appearance of a frontal view of a person's head and shoulders. Such patterns are generally seen as indicating a coming market decline.

Heavy: Term used to describe the market or a stock when it fails to rally as briskly as would be liked.

Hedge Fund: A fund which is allowed to sell stocks short.

Hedging: A process whereby one buys or sells a financial instrument, normally an option or a future, as a protective measure to counterbalance another investment. If one owns a stock, for example, one can hedge by buying a put with an exercise price below the present price of the stock.

Held – Not Held: Terms used to denote two types of "market orders." A not-held order allows the floor broker more discretion in determining when he will and will not execute the order than does a held order which must be executed immediately without price restrictions. See *Market Order* and *Limit Order*.

Highs – New Highs: Terms used to refer to stocks trading either in an all time high or a new high for the year; usually the latter.

Hipshooter: See *Gun Slinger.*

House: Common name given to brokerage institutions.

Income: Term usually used to refer to dividend income that a stock pays or the interest that a bond pays in contrast to moneys made through capital gains.

Index: Term used to refer to any of the more common "averages" used to measure stock prices, such as the Standard and Poors Index, The New York Stock Exchange Index, or the Dow Jones Index.

Index Fund: A fund which attempts to duplicate the major market indexes such as the Dow or the Standard and Poors indexes. Most such funds are governed by some variation of the Efficient Market theory of the stock market.

In the Money: Another phrase used in connection with options to indicate that the underlying stock is selling at a price above the exercise price of a call option and under the exercise price of a put option. See *Out of the Money.*

Institution: Term used to refer to Mutual Funds, Bank trust department, etc. Used to distinguish supposedly large sophisticated investors from individual investors.

Institutional Broker: Adjective used commonly on Wall Street supposedly to separate those who deal with lay investors from those who deal with funds, trust departments, etc. In fact, used more to locate someone in the class structure of the market than to define actual function.

Investor: Term used to distinguish those who buy stocks for a quick capital gain (speculator) from those who buy for income and long term growth. Also term used by speculators to define themselves when they have bought a stock that hasn't worked out.

Lettered Stock: Restricted stock of a company which cannot be freely traded. Such stocks generally have the same value as the traded stock, but since they cannot be traded, often sell at a discount.

Lift: An upward movement in the market after a decline. The term lift is used more often to signify an interday upward movement. See also *Technical Rally/Decline*.

Limit order: A buy or sell order which is placed with a specific price attached to it. For example, a sell order at 45 which means that it cannot be sold for less than 45.

Listed Stock: Stock which is registered with one of the major exchanges and traded on the Exchange. This generally means either the New York Stock Exchange or the American Stock Exchange.

Liquidity: (1) When used in reference to a specific company refers to the cash flow of the company in relation to its cash needs. A company may have sufficient assets to cover liabilities but still have a cash flow, i.e., liquidity problem.

(2) When used to refer to the market itself refers to the volume of trading characteristic of a stock. A stock which trades in low volume is considered to have low liquidity. Fundamentalists are more interested in the first type of liquidity, traders in the second.

Load/No-Load: Terms used to distinguish between different types of mutual funds. The Load type entails an upfront charge when you buy into the fund whereas a No-load fund does not.

Long Term Profits/Losses: Profits and/or losses incurred on stocks owned for a sufficient period of time (in the past, six months, presently, a year) which allowed them to be treated as long term capital gains or losses for income tax purposes.

Loss: Something which no one on Wall Street likes to talk about.

Margin: The amount of money that must be put up in buying a stock. Margin varies with economic and market conditions. In recent years it has fluctuated between 50 per cent and 75 per cent which means that one must put up 50 per cent of the value of the stock bought or 75 per cent of the value of the stock bought.

Margin call: If a stock that one has bought on the margin declines in price, one may receive a margin call which requires that the owner of stock put up more money or be forced to sell the stock.

Market order: An order to buy or sell a stock immediately without price restrictions. See *Limit Order.*

Momentum: A market concept based on the notion that the stock market tends to continue to move in the direction in which it is moving.

Money manager: Label given to those persons who run portfolios for wealthy individuals or institutions.

Most Active List: Exactly what it says: the list of those stocks which have traded in the most volume during a specific period of time.

Move: Either an advance or decline of a stock or the stock market as a whole of some significance.

Multiple: See P/E.

Mutual Fund: See *Fund, Closed-End Fund, Open-End Fund.*

Naked Option: Refers to an option which is sold without the seller owning the underlying stock.

Negotiated commissions: Since May 1, 1975, member firms of the New York Stock Exchange can offer discounts to customers if they so wish. This has given rise to what is now called negotiated commissions.

New York Stock Exchange: The largest stock exchange located on Wall Street and Broad in New York City.

New York Stock Exchange Index: An index based upon all of the stocks traded on the New York Stock Exchange. Probably, the most broadly based index used.

Nifty-fifty: Label given to the fifty major companies which are the current favorites of institutional investors. Most of these companies are very large corporate institutions, but they also include a relatively high number of high multiple glamor stocks.

Odd lot; Odd lotter: Name given to trades and individuals who trade in less than one hundred share units. The odd lotter is often used as a contrary index by technicians, i.e., when the odd lotter is buying, the market is going to go down and vice versa.

Open ended fund: A fund, generally a mutual fund, which is constantly attempting to raise more capital. It is considered an open ended fund since there is no limit on the amount of money which can be invested through the fund. See *Closed Fund.*

Option: An option is the right to either buy or sell a stock at a fixed price for a specific period of time.

Out of the Money: Phrase used to denote an option whose underlying stock is trading under the options exercise price in the case of a Call and above its exercise price in the case of a Put option.

Over the Counter: This market functions differently from the New York Stock Exchange and the American Stock Exchange. Stocks are sold through and bought from dealer brokers rather than through specialists. Most smaller companies trade in the OTC market since the capitalization requirements are much less than those of the major exchanges.

Paper: See *Commercial Paper.*

Portfolio: Refers to the actual holdings, i.e., stocks, bonds, etc., in a given account.

Preferred stock: A class of stock with priority rights over common stock in securing its dividend, which is normally specified. Preferred stocks normally also have priority rights over common stock to assets in case of liquidation.

Premium: Refers to value in excess of the face value of a bond and/or the value in excess of the exercise price of an option.

P/E: (Price-earning ratio) The ratio of the price of a stock divided by the annual per share earnings of the company. Most people consider a P/E between 8 and 12 as fairly standard with lower or higher P/E indicating either expectations of dramatically higher earnings or lower earnings in the future.

Prime; prime rate: The interest rate set by banks for their best customers.

Public: Used to refer to all those who are not professionally involved in the market. More recently the "public" is often contrasted with "institutional" participants.

Put: An option to sell a stock at a set price for a specified period of time.

Quality: Adjective generally applied to companies and their stock which are seen to have superior management, a record of good earnings, and a record of consistent dividend payments.

Quote: Term used to denote the present price of a stock, normally coupled with the bid/ask prices.

Rally: A fairly rapid upward movement in the market, more often than not following a significant decline.

Random Walk: Phrase used most by Efficient Market theorists to indicate that there is no discernible pattern to a series of events such as stock prices. The implication is that it is a purely random affair whether a stock will go up or down at any moment.

Registered Representative: The official New York Stock Exchange term for brokers.

Research Department: What every brokerage house claims to have.

Resistance Area: Phrase used to refer to price level where the market as a whole or a specific stock has in the past run into heavy selling pressure which has prevented the stock or the market as a whole to move higher in price. See *Support Level.*

Return / rate of return: Term used to refer to total gains including capital appreciation and dividends or yield from an investment.

Rights: See *Warrants.*

Seat: Term used to refer to membership in a given exchange, i.e., "a seat on the New York Exchange."

SEC: The Securities Exchange Commission. The federal government regulatory agency responsible for overseeing the market.

Service: (1)Term used to refer to the numerous brokerage functions that are not directly related to executing orders, i.e., supplying recommendations, checking out a specific company, evaluating a portfolio, etc.
(2) Used to refer to any of a number of market advisory services from the Value Line letter to any of the here-today, gone-tomorrow market letters.

Short: To sell a stock that one does not own in the anticipation that it will go lower and allow one to buy it back for less money than one sold it at. To sell short, one must be able to borrow the stock. One will usually borrow from the brokerage house with whom one does business.

Short Interest: Indicator which reveals the number of shares that have been sold short in a particular company and the market as a whole. Many consider a large short interest to be bullish since it indicates that there is a large demand for stocks since every short seller has sold a stock without owning it. See also *Boxing* for another variation of this procedure.

Short Term Profits / Losses: Refers to capital gains or losses which result from sale of stock held for a period of less than a year. Such profits and losses are treated like unearned income for tax purposes.

Shot / to take a shot: Expression used to indicate a more speculative investment.

Sideways Market: A market which can't make up its mind whether it wants to go up or down.

Small Investor: Generally considered to be any investor with annual income of under $25,000 and a portfolio of under $10,000.

Source: Term used to refer to persons who are considered to have types of 'inside' or other "good" information. Nearly every professional in the market relies to some extent upon a "source" or two.

Specialist: A member of the exchange who is given the responsibility by the exchange to make a market in a particular stock.

Specialist's Book: The book which a specialist keeps which records the various buy and sell orders that he has been given at prices either above or below the market. See *Limit Order*.

Speculator: Term used to distinguish those people who buy stocks primarily for capital gains rather than for income. Speculators are also normally interested in short term gains.

Splits: When a stock is divided into any number of shares to adjust its price to a range which is considered preferable. A stock which has gone from 20 to 40 may be split two for one to bring its price back to 20. Sometimes there are reverse splits where a stock which has gone from 5 to 1 may be reissued at a 5 for 1 ratio to bring it back to 5. There are many different types of splits: 3 for 2, 5 for 4, etc.

Spread: Refers to any of a number of different strategies for simutaneously purchasing and selling different option series associated with a given stock.

Squeeze; Short Squeeze: Term used to describe situation where an upward movement in the price of a stock puts pressure upon those who have sold the stock short. In such situations short sellers may be forced to cover their position forcing the stock up further thereby repeating the process for those who have shorted the stock at a higher price.

Stop/Loss Order: A popular trading technique among traders in which a specific price below the current market for a stock is selected (a price which the trader feels for any of a number of reasons should not be penetrated by the stock) where the stock is to be automatically sold.

Story: Information which is more than a tip, but less than confirmed; to some, the lifeblood of the market.

Straddle: Refers to the trading strategy of buying or selling an equivalent number of puts or calls on a given underlying stock with the same exercise price and expiration date.

Street Account: Phrase used to denote customer accounts where the stocks are kept in the firm name. To protect the firm such accounts are necessary when stocks are bought on margin. Many customers also prefer such accounts because it cuts down on paper work.

Striking Price: See *Exercise Price*.

Support level: Expression used to indicate that at a certain price below the present price of a stock or the market as a whole, there exists significant buy orders which will not allow the stock to drop below that price. While the concept of support levels is associated most often with Cyclist-Chartists, pretty much all market participants "believe" in a variety of support levels.

Symbol: The letter combinations which are used to denote a company on the tape.

Take Over: Phrase used to describe process whereby one company takes control of another company, usually by buying the stock of the 'taken over' company through a special offering for the outstanding stock of the company being acquired.

Tape: The ongoing and generally up to the minute record of all stock transactions. At one time it truly was a tape with each exchange publishing its own tape. Today, it is more likely to be an electronic board with the transactions of all exchanges trading in a particular stock combined. Sometimes also used to refer to the ongoing "publication" of the various news service, Dow Jones and Reuters.

Tax Selling: Expression used to categorize selling which is seen to be due to a desire to take losses in a given taxable year to offset gains. December is a month in which there is usually a good deal of tax selling.

Technical Rally/Decline: A rally in what is generally considered to be a down market or a decline in an up market which is due not so much to a change in the market, but rather to the fact that the market never goes straight down or up.

Ten K/10K: Refers to more detailed financial form that

must be filed with the Security and Exchange Commission. Many persons consider these forms to be much more accurate statements of a company's financial position than their annual reports.

Test: The market is generally seen as "testing" previous lows or highs when it approaches in price these previous lows or highs. See *Support Level.*

Third Market: Expression used to refer to those transactions involving listed stocks between large institutional houses which do not go through the exchange, but are rather direct transactions between the buying and selling parties. Such transactions are normally executed through an OTC firm. When there is no OTC firm participation such transactions are often referred to as constituting a Fourth Market.

Ticker: See *Tape.*

Top: Term used to denote the high prices set by the market. As with the concept of market bottom, technicians often refer to double and triple tops. See *Resistance Area.*

Trader: A market participant who moves in and out of the market often and with speed. See chapter 5.

Trading Room: Term used to refer to that segment of a firm where orders are usually executed. A salesman will forward his order to his trading room which will in turn forward the order to the floor of the exchange, i.e., their person on the floor. It is the responsibility of the trading room to get the best possible execution for any order; to do this it must keep in constant touch with what is going on within the exchanges themselves.

Transaction: A market trade.

Two Dollar Broker: A floor broker who will trade for another brokerage house for a set two dollar commission per hundred shares. Many smaller brokerage houses with a limited number of floor brokers make use of such persons. See *Floor Broker*.

Unlisted Stock: A publicly held company which is not listed and, therefore, not traded on an existing exchange. Often used to refer, however, to stocks which are only listed and traded in the Over the Counter market.

Up and Away: The Put counterpart to a Down and Out, i.e., a 'limited risk put option' sold normally for a six months period at a variable premium which becomes void if the underlying stock appreciates by 10 per cent or more.

Volatility: Refers to the degree to which a stock moves up and down relative to its price. A stock which tends to go up and down regularly is considered to be a highly volatile stock whereas one that does not is considered to be non-volatile. See also *Beta*.

Volume: Refers to the number of shares traded in a given period of time.

Warrants: Rights to buy a stock at a certain price. Warrants are issued by the company itself to present stock holders, often in lieu of dividends. In many ways they are like a call option but they are issued by the company itself and are rights to company held stock rather than to stock already being traded.

Window Dressing: Expression used to refer to the fairly common practice of institutional funds whereby the fund sells and buys stocks near the end of a quarter in order to improve the appearance of their portfolio. They will sell a stock which has performed poorly thereby not having to show that they owned it and will buy stocks which have done well, giving the impression that they were very astute. In actuality, such window-dressing cannot only not make money, but also can cost money; many fund managers, however, feel that it helps sales of the fund.

Wiplash Wipsaw: Terms used to refer to a situation where a stock moves in one direction and then suddenly moves strongly in the other direction. More common among highly volatile stocks. This term is usually only used to refer to situations where one has bought the stock in an upward movement only to see it then go down, or has shorted the stock in the downward movement only to see it then go up.

Yield: Term used to refer to dividend or interest paid on a security.

Appendix C: A Theoretical and Methodological Note

From a theoretical perspective this book could be considered an empirical study in the sociology of knowledge,[1] though I prefer to consider it an empirical study in the sociology of mind.[2] I see the sociology of mind as similar to the sociology of knowledge in that its primary focus is the worldviews and common sense perspectives of everyday life. It is further similar in that it shows how these different worldviews are capable of generating different "realities", which in turn can lead to different actions; and it also attempts to locate these worldviews within a social context. Where the sociology of knowledge emphasizes the relationships among specific perspectives and specific social positions, the sociology of mind emphasizes the social parameters of thought and mind itself. In this respect the sociology of mind has more in common with Max Weber's interest in different forms of rationality[3] and Jurgen Habermas's notion of various types of 'cognitive interests.'[4] That is, the sociology of mind is more concerned with forms of thought than the specific content of thought. It is, however, most definitely a sociological concern rather than a purely philosophical or psychological one, in that it sees these forms of thought as having social roots.

Though I earlier referred to this book as an empirical study in the sociology of mind, I should like to stress that this study was neither undertaken nor pursued in order to generate empirical support for a theoretical position. It rather grew out of a genuine personal interest in the stock market. Admittedly, as a theoretically orientated sociologist, I always approached the market with various theoretical questions in mind, but it was the market itself which stimulated this study more than anything else. Whatever theoretical status it may have, therefore, it is primarily an empirical study based on (1) over three thousand hours of participant observation (by this I mean structured participant observation not simply watching the market) carried out over a period of twelve years; (2) two series of formal interviews, numbering thirty and forty-five respectively, with specifically selected market professionals; and (3) an ongoing, analytically critical relationship with one particular stock market professional who served as a prime informer.[5]

I emphasize this last relationship for two reasons: first, though I established contacts, both formal and informal, with numerous market professionals, for example stock brokers, partners in brokerage firms, market analysts, fund managers, and private investors, none of those relationships even approached this one in terms of the amount or the quality of information I was able to obtain. Secondly, and more importantly, though I was fairly open regarding the nature and substance of my research with the various market people I met, talked with, and observed, I did not engage them in the types of explicit theoretical discussions which were common between myself and my prime informer.[6]

It is nearly impossible to judge the relative importance of these various sources of information. If, however, I had to quantify them I would say that the study is based fifty per-cent upon participant observation, twenty-five per-cent upon formal interviews, and twenty-five per-cent upon my prime informer. There were a number of the other factors, however, which had a bearing on my ability to obtain this information and which deserve a brief comment.

Throughout my research I ran continually into four major problems: (1) gaining entry; (2) establishing trust; (3) obtaining verification; and (4) maintaining autonomy.[7]

Gaining entry is a very real problem when doing a study such as this. Most market professionals have a fairly skeptical view of social scientists. They have no good reason to talk to a sociologist or a social-psychologist; their time is worth money to them; moreover they are not very eager to share their view of the market, which is often fairly critical, with a stranger. Most firms are even less eager to have anyone snooping around.

It became apparent very early that I could not simply walk into a brokerage firm and hope to interview anyone. I might have tried to pass myself off as a potential customer, but for professional ethical reasons, I could not do this. Moreover, I doubt that I would have been able to get the type of information I wanted if I was seen as a potential customer. What I needed was some sort of sponsorship. When it came to interviewing institutional salesmen, management personnel and money managers, sponsorship proved indispensable.

In order to obtain sponsorship, I relied almost exclusively on referrals from persons I had already interviewed. In nearly all cases, it was further necessary that the person referring me be either a close personal friend of the new informer or someone in a position of authority. Those in positions of authority proved most useful.

The numer of interviews I was able to generate through personal contacts averaged between one and two. When starting with men of influence, I was able to average four or five new interviews. Consequently, I spent a great deal of time trying to develop contacts with persons of influence. I was seldom able to convert initial contacts into formal interviews. In fact, about eighty per cent of the time these people were rather interviewing me to determine whether they would sponsor me in interviewing others.

In order to obtain their sponsorship, I had to convince them: (1) that I was not out to cause trouble or simply to do a muckraking job on the market; (2) that I would not violate any confidences; and (3) that I knew something about the market. In most cases, I was able to relieve their mind regarding points one and two by referring them to mutual acquaintances. More often than not, such persons had made it possible for me to be granted this first interview. Point three, in most cases, however, proved to be the most important criterion. It was generally only when I was able to show that I was familiar with the market and the way it worked that I was able to acquire new sponsorship. I was never tested in a formal way. It was rather necessary for me to prove in informal conversation that I understood the market and moreover that I liked it. I had to show that I was already a "market insider", and I am quite sure that if I hadn't been able to do this, fewer doors would have been opened to me. It almost seemed to be the case that if I already knew what I knew, no harm could come from my learning a little bit more.

The need to show that I was familiar with the way the market worked was even more important in the actual interviewing process. It was crucial in developing the sense of trust required if I was to get meaningful responses. Again and again for the first ten minutes to half hour, I found my interviewee fencing with me. They would hedge their answers and ask me to explain in more detail what I was trying to do. Many would also question me as to who I was working for and what I intended to do with the information I was collecting. They wanted to be assured that everything they told me would be confidential. As I was able to show that I was familiar with what they were doing and what they were saying, however, nearly all adopted a different attitude. In some cases, this would happen after I had discussed a particular stock which the interviewee had mentioned; in other cases, it seemed to occur more as a result of the way I formulated my question – how I used the market terminology.

Interestingly, once this occurred most interviewees opened up completely. In fact, many prolonged what was basically an hour interview, into a two hour discussion. The one group which tended to maintain their reserve was the Firm Salesmen.

This, I think, was primarily due to their fears that I was, in fact, working for the firm in some capacity or other. In most cases, I found it difficult to restrain my interviewees and so complete my interview.

Though most people were finally willing to talk openly with me, I soon found I had a problem of verification. Many of those I talked with had a tendency to exaggerate their own success in the market and the job they were doing for their customers. In some cases, I had other contacts, often in management, which I could use for verification. Such contacts, however, were of limited use since I could not very well get up in the middle of an interview to check out what I was being told, in order to insure that I was getting a true story. Furthermore, I was hesitant to use such contacts since they would have in a way violated my commitment of confidentiality. I found, however, that the more I was able to convince the person I was interviewing that I was familiar with the market, the less likely that they would try to impress me. More than once the person I was interviewing began to give me an honest story only after I had caught him in a misstatement of some sort. A classic example of this was a broker who had originally told me that he was heavily invested in one of the market's standout stocks, only to be ignorant of the last quarterly earnings of that company. 'Well, I'm really not that heavily into it. One or two of my customers have a few hundred shares.' Rather than being hostitle towards me as a result of such interchanges, most became even more engaging and more direct.

My last problem was that of maintaining autonomy. This was not a general problem, but it did arise a number of times. On a few occasions I was approached to feed back information that I had acquired. Sometimes it was no more than a request that I give my opinion as to whether I thought the person I had interviewed would work out or not. On one occasion I was even offered the right to look over some monthly production figures in return for such information. In all cases, I refused to offer any such opinions, with the result that in one case I became persona non grata. I mention this point only because such offers are very attractive when doing a study of this sort; given the need for sponsorship, it is very difficult to turn one's back on individuals who can open doors for you. Fortunately, I had by that time established enough contacts so that I could afford to lose a few. If I had confronted such a dilemma early in my research the temptations would have been much greater.

In summary, I found that the essential element of such a study is that one must already be very familiar with the subject matter. For some types of research professional degrees are sufficient to open the right doors. In the case of the market, they are not and I would guess that they are not in most situations where one is dealing with people of influence and wealth. They are simply not impressed; in fact, they may very well be put off. From a theoretical position, this is a generally known point; in practice, however, it is too often ignored.

NOTES

Chapter 1

1. See APPENDIX B for definition of market terms used in text.

2. The issue of the intentionality of knowledge has been discussed and analysed by many. I would recommend my own *A Critique of Sociological Reasoning*, (Totowa: 1979); Karl Mannheim's *Ideology and Utopia* (Part I) (New York: Harvest Books, 1936); and Berger and Luckmann, *The Social Construction of Reality* (New York: 1967). That there are different types of interests is a related but analytically distinct question. In addition to the works just cited, see Habermas, *Knowledge and Human Interest* (Boston: 1971).

3. There is, of course, nothing peculiar about the market in this respect. All meanings are social by definition and are based upon some sort of consensus. This issue is discussed at length in books by Mannheim, Berger and Luckmann, and Smith, *op. cit.*

4. See Berger and Luckmann, *op. cit.*, pp. 117*ff.*

5. My use of the term "true believer" is meant to imply an intellectual position, but one which serves as the grounds for action.

Chapter 2

1. It is difficult to make broad generalizations regarding preferences for general economic news versus financial news when discussing true Fundamentalists. My experience indicates, however, that while most who claim to be Fundamentalists indicate a preference for strictly financial news, most true Fundamentalists are more concerned with general economic news.

2. Bill Chester's selling tends to be more intensive because he accumulates stock over a period of time. When he feels his stocks are fully valued, however, he wants to get out as quickly as possible.

Chapter 3

1. It is difficult to generalize about institutional salesmen, because their role varies from firm to firm. Generally, the larger the firm, the more analysts, the more block traders, etc., the more peripheral the institutional salesman is to the actual buying and selling of stocks. In smaller operations, the salesman may actually be involved in the execution of market orders.

2. Providing female companionship as well as food and drink represents one of the seamier sides of the market. Because most involved in this type of behavior don't like to talk about it, it is difficult to know how extensive

it is. From my experience, I would judge the practice to be no more nor less common than it is in any "sales relationship" where substantial sums of money are involved and "customer service" plays an important role.

Chapter 4

1. It is this belief in an underlying order to the market which separates Bob Klein and other true Cyclist-Chartists from those who simply make use of technical information. This point will be developed in more detail in analysing the technically orientated salesmen of the market.

2. Bob Klein is fairly extreme in this regard even for a Cyclist-Chartist. A number of persons who qualify as true Cyclist-Chartists favor a more probabilistic view towards their charts and consequently are more willing to admit that their charts may be wrong at times.

Chapter 5

1. If John Holland has a "market bible" it would be G. M. Loeb's *The Battle for Investment Survival* (New York: Simon & Schuster, 1957)

2. Or, more accurately, 'buy low, sell when fairly valued.'

Chapter 6

1. This is, of course, true for true believers who are also brokers except for the fact that a true believer, by definition, must also do pretty well in the market itself.

2. See the *1980 Fact Book* of the New York Stock Exchange, p. 58. It is difficult to generalize from their figures to all firms, because not all firms are equally involved in underwriting and firm trading, i.e., trading firm money. In some firms these activities may each account for twenty-five per cent of the firm's gross earnings while in other firms they may account for practically nothing. Percentages vary from year to year.

3. For an interesting, if somewhat biased view, of this issue see *The Registered Representative: A Look Above the Bottom Line*, (The New York Stock Exchange: May, 1975).

4. See the Security and Exchange Committee's *Special Study, op.cit.* A summary of the revised rules can also be obtained from the SEC as well as from the various exchanges and a number of brokerage houses.

5. See *The Registered Representative: A Look Above the Bottom Line, op. cit.*

6. I am here referring to the impact of the four intentional dimensions discussed briefly in the first chapter. This issue will be analysed in greater detail in chapter 15.

Chapter 10

1. There is a significant amount of feedback in this situation. Both Customer Salesmen and Action Salesmen, as well as Traders, tend to favor the more active stocks, since they account for a good deal of market activity.

Chapter 12

1. For a level headed, non-technical treatment of the Efficient Theory of the Market Theory, plus an extensive bibliography see Burton G. Malkiel, *A Random Walk Down Wall Street,* (New York: Norton, 1973).

2. The introduction of negotiated rates and the growth of discount houses could dramatically change the market role of people like Dave Gibbons. These developments, coupled with the ever increasing number of research reports and the more rapid dissemination of information, have greatly strengthened the position of both the Efficient Market theorists and those willing to function as Order Takers. It is unlikely that these types will ever become dominant within the traditional Wall Street firms or institutions, but if discount houses and index funds succeed, there are bound to be many more of these types in the future than there are today.

Chapter 13

1. Findings based on my own data and N.Y.S.E. reports. See *NYSE Registered Representative* published by the New York Stock Exchange (one pamphlet covers 1967, 1968, and 1969; another 1970 and 1971) and *The Registered Representative, op. cit.*

2. See pamphlets noted in Note 1. The major data I am drawing upon here, however, is taken from my own series of interviews and my field notes.

3. This "non-deterministic" quality does not mean that the market lacks ordering principles, but only that such principles are not actualized in all situations. The market like other forms of social life is governed by underlying "structures" which "compete" with each other at the level of concrete events. For more detailed discussions of this important philosophical issue, see Roy Bhaskar, *The Possibilities of Naturalism* (New York, 1979), Rom Harré *Social Being* (Totowa, 1980), Rom Harré and Paul Secord, *The Explanation of Social Behavior* (Totowa: 1972) and Anthony Giddens, *New Rules of Sociological Method* (New York: 1976).

4. Though the market is always 'changing', it has undergone changes of a more uncommon sort during the last few years. More specifically, it has become more institutional, i.e., more and more transactions are being carried on for institutional investors rather than individual investors. It has also become more computerized.

Increased volume has created back office problems for many firms; some firms have also had liquidity problems. Many firms have been forced to merge. The various exchanges themselves are being pressured to merge their operations in various ways. The traditional role of the floor specialist has come under increased scrutiny. Negotiated rates have been introduced; a third market has emerged. For the most part, however, these changes have been structural rather than ideological. That is, they have not dramatically affected the basic overviews of the market nor the various types who make up the market. This is why they have received relatively little attention in this book.

5. This attitude is consistent with what Ben Decker had to say regarding the need for market professionals to be bullish. From my own observations I

would say that there is much truth in this view. I am reminded of one advisory service which took a decidedly bearish position in the early seventies; it put all of its accounts into cash. Despite their relative success, I know of at least three accounts that they lost through refusing to play the market.

Chapter 14

1. For a general discussion, see Charles W. Smith, *op. cit.* pp. 62-67.

2. The fact that true believers are less susceptable to the pull of the crowd explains more than anything else why they generally do better in the market than others. The real strength of a true believer is not his particular view of the market but rather his commitment to a particular view of the market which makes him relatively immune to the pull of the crowd. It is not that he is always, or even usually, right, but that he manages to avoid being disastrously wrong. This has important implications for the small investor. He doesn't have to be a genius; he only needs to avoid being a fool. For those interested in the general implications of this study for the small investor, see APPENDIX A "Some Practical Advice to the Individual Investor" p. 155.

Chapter 15

1. What could be called a fourth theme has been the role of experts in defining social reality. The theme was introduced in the beginning of this study (see pp. 22-23). What we have discovered as with so much else is that expertise varies as objectives change. With the exception of the crowd, however, we have seen that there are always experts of some sort, and even in the case of the crowd there is the assumption that such experts exist.

2. The literature on this subject is too great even to list. For a general discussion of the issue see the first part of my *Critique of Sociological Reasoning op. cit.* Also Habermas, *op. cit.*, and his *Communication and the Evolution of Society* (Boston: 1979); and Max Weber, *The Theory of Social and Economic Organization,* trans. Talcott Parsons (New York: 1947) pp. 88-118.

3. Early in this study I recognized that the different market philosophies I was encountering could be classified in terms of my four basic intentional dimensions; I consequently began to use the notions of Fundamentalist, Insider, Cyclist-Chartist, and Trader in structuring my research. It was not till much later that I became aware that these same dimensions could be used to classify the way people made use of these overviews.

4. The first view as indicated in the text is basically that of the pragmatic school. It is also that of what generally passes as the scientific view and the 'realist' view. It similarly has much in common with the Weberian concept of means-ends rationality. The ideological view meanwhile is better reflected in what may be called the interpretive schools covering everything from phenomenology to hermeneutic thought. The cognitive view has historically been primarily associated with pure philosophy and philosophical

theology, though it is also the view of many cognitive psychologists. The last view could be called the classical sociological view being drawn primarily from Durkheim.

Appendix A

1. This advice applies only to the New York Stock Exchange, since all stop orders on the America Exchange are automatically stop-limit orders. A stop order at 45 will only be executed at 45.

Appendix C:

1. For what is perhaps the classic formulation of the sociology of knowledge see *Ideology and Utopia,* Karl Mannheim (New York: 1936). For a more recent statement see *The Social Construction of Reality,* Peter Berger and Thomas Luckmann (New York: 1967).

2. For a preliminary discussion see *A Critique of Sociological Reasoning,* Charles W. Smith (Oxford: 1979).

3. Weber's concern with "rationality" runs throughout his writings. See especially, however, his *The Theory of Social and Economic Organization,* (New York: 1947) and his *Sociology of Religion,* (Boston: 1963).

4. See the Appendix, "Knowledge and Human Interest" in his *Knowledge and Human Interest,* (Boston, 1971) and his *Legitimation Crisis,* (Boston: 1975).

5. The use of prime informers has historically been a major source of sociological data through such sources are often not explicitly noted. Whole studies have been based upon such sources; see, for example, *The Professional Thief,* Edwin H. Sutherland, (Chicago: 1937). More normally the prime informer is one source in what is basically a participant observation study; perhaps the classic example of this is William F. Whyte's use of Doc in *Street Corner Society,* (Chicago: 1955).

6. By "fairly open" I mean that I never engaged in any form of subterfuge; I quite openly explained that I was interested in understanding how different market participants interpreted and understood the market. I did not, however, normally present my own types nor any of my more theoretical observations.

7. For a description of similar problems confronted by a person doing a similar type study, see *The Gamesman,* Michael Maccoby, (New York: Simon and Schuster, 1976). Relying, as he did, more upon formal interviews and less upon participant observation, Maccoby was forced to rely more than I upon persons of influence. For what is perhaps the classic statement on participant observation, see William F. Whyte, *op. cit.*, pp. 299ff.

Index

(Glossary items are not automatically listed in this index. Cross Referencing is, therefore, advised. Indexed items which appear in the Glossary are marked with an asterisk).

Action, market action,* 14, 58-59, 99, 103
Action Salesmen, 76, 99-105, 151
Ambiguity, market ambiguity, 11-29, 66, 135, 141-142, 145
Analysts,* 13, 42, 53, 69

Barrons, 34, 161
Berger, Peter, 211, 215
Bhaskar, Roy, 213
Brokers, attitude toward,* 15-17, 35, 62. See *Professionals* and *Experts*
Business Week, 161
Buying and Selling, 13, 21, 50, 75, 100, 137-141, 168; attitudes toward, 14-16, 37-38, 48-49, 111; Brokers' own, 14-16, 37, 45, 53, 62, 83, 91, 96, 102, 163. See *Short Selling*

Charts, chart services,* See *Market Services* and *Technical Information*
Churning,* 18
Class Characteristics, class impact, 14, 15, 125-126
Commissions,* 17-18, 36, 62, 69-70, 86, 113,150,172
Confidence, 19-20,36, 53, 63, 74, 78, 94, 112
Confidence Index, 34
Confidentiality, 14, 28, 207-209
Contacts, market contacts, 42, 44, 62, 85-86, 91, 112, 127; in doing study, 209. See *Methodology*
Crowd, crowd syndrome, 131, 133-143, 151, 167. See *Psychological influences*
Customers, attitude towards, 35-36, 40, 43, 49, 63, 81-82, 87-88, 103, 112, 120
Customer Salesmen, 76, 85-91, 151
Cyclist-Chartist, Cyclist-chartist view, 23, 24, 28, 47-56, 75, 126-128, 145, 147, 148, 151

'Defining the Situation', 22, 134
Discount House,* 97, 213
Dodd, David L., 34, 161
Dow, the Dow,* 34
Durkheim, Emile, 215

E. F. Hutton, 173
Economic factors, attitude toward economic factors, 33-34, 48, 59, 78, 113, 211. See *Fundamentalists*
Efficient Market Theory,* 15, 116, 119-121, 213. See *Index Fund*
Ethical Questions and Issues, 19, 91. See *Methodology*
Experts, expertise, 12-13, 16, 23, 48, 54, 70, 119, 209. See *Professionals*

Fed, the Federal Reserve Bank,* 44
Federal regulations, see *Regulations*
Firm Salesmen, 76, 77-84, 151
Forbes, 34, 161
Fortune, 34, 161
Fundamentalists, Fundamentalist view, 23, 24, 28, 33-40, 75, 78, 126-128, 145-146, 148, 151

Gambling, 14, 35, 99. See *Risk*
Giddens, Anthony, 208
Glamour, glamour stocks,* see *Growth*
Graham, Ben, 34, 161
Greed, 51, 82, 88, 112, 169
Growth, growth stocks,* 34, 45, 61, 101, 212

Habermas, Jurgen, 205, 211, 214, 215
Harré, Rom, 213
Headhunting, 89

Index Fund,* 15, 119. See *Efficient Market Theory*
Information, sources of and attitude towards: 21, 35-36, 42, 45, 59, 60, 86, 88-90, 112-113, 118, 169; for study,

206-207
Insiders, Insider view, 23, 24, 28, 41-46, 75, 86, 126-128, 145-146, 148, 151-154
Institutional investors, brokers,* See *Professionals*
Intentional modes, modalities, 24, 66, 75-76, 148
Interpretation, 21-23, 35
Interviewing, 207, 208. See *Methodology*

Knowledge, market knowledge, 14, 16, 20, 23-24, 36, 48-49, 70, 82, 94, 120, 136, 152, 160-161, 174; self-knowledge, 165-166, 169-171. See also *Sociology of Knowledge* and *Experts*

Loeb, Gerald, 16, 212
Luckmann, Thomas, 211, 215

Maccoby, Michael, 215
Malkiel, Burton G., 213
Management, attitudes, future in, attitude towards, 14, 16-17, 33, 73, 78, 84, 89-90, 95, 96, 102-103, 104, 115
Manipulation, 43, 71, 113, 116
Mannheim, Karl, 211, 215
Margin,* 82, 114
Market Professionals, See *Professionals*
Market Salesmen, 76, 93-97, 151
Market Services, 12, 34, 93-94, 97, 163. See *Technical Approach*
Mass Psychology, See *Crowd, crowd syndrome* and *Psychological influences.*
Merrill Lynch, 173
Methodology, 205-210
Money Managers,* 13, 15, 69, 117, 119, 130. See *Professionals*
Mutual Funds,* 158-160

New York Stock Exchange, 9, 94, 126
New York Times, 34, 113, 161
Newsweek, 34

Odd Lots, odd lotters,* 50, 113, 163
Options,* 37, 41, 82, 128, 129, 163, 176, 178
O.T.C., over the counter stocks, market,* 101, 128, 129

Parsons, Talcott, 214
Participant Observation, 206, 215. See *Methodology*
Prime Informer, 206, 215. See *Methodology*
Professionals, market professionals, 13-14, 20, 23-24, 69-70, 125, 142; attitude towards, 15, 120. See *Experts*
Psychological influences, 52, 55, 85, 100, 169. See *Crowd, crowd syndrome*

Rationalizers, 104-105, 109-110, 126-127, 147, 149, 150, 151
Recommendations, 18, 35, 38, 59, 61, 73, 75, 77-79, 101
Regulations, rules, 43-44, 71, 91, 103
Research, attitude towards research, 14, 39, 42, 79-80, 88-89
Risk, 18, 37, 51, 63, 82-83, 101, 165. See *Gambling*

Salesmen, 24-25, 69-76, 79, 126-127, 147, 149, 150, 151, 164
Secord, Paul, 213
"Self-fulfilling Prophesy", 21-22, 24, 145
Selling, see *Buying and Selling*
Short Loss,* 60, 166, 174
Short Selling,* 37, 50, 52-53, 60, 64, 114
Small Investor, See *Customers*
'Smith, Adam', 161
Social Class, See *Class Characteristics*
Sociology of Knowledge, 23, 205
Sociology of Mind, 152-155, 205-206
Specialist,* 64, 130, 138
Sponsorship, stock, 45, 52, 59, 61; personal sponsorship, 207-210
Sutherland, Edwin H., 215

Tape, the tape,* 52, 64, 100
Technical Approach, technical information,* 18, 34, 49, 55, 59, 80, 118, 163. See *Cyclist-Chartist view*
Time, 34
Trader, Trader view,* 23, 24, 28, 57-65, 75, 126-128, 145, 147, 148, 151
True Believer(s), 24-25, 65-66, 72, 75, 126-127, 130, 136, 149-150, 151, 164, 212, 214

U.S. News and World Reports, 34

Wall Street Journal, 12, 13, 34, 113, 161
Wall Street Week, 13
Weber, Max, 205, 214, 215
Work, work ethic, attitude toward work, 17, 36, 39, 44, 48, 52, 57, 60
Whyte, William F., 215

D0053374